GAME DAY
NEBRASKA FOOTBALL

GAME DAY
NEBRASKA FOOTBALL

**The Greatest Games, Players, Coaches and Teams
in the Glorious Tradition of Cornhusker Football**

TRIUMPH
BOOKS
CHICAGO

Athlon Sports
AMERICA'S PREMIER SPORTS ANNUALS

Library of Congress Control Number: 2006901591

This book is available in quantity at special discounts for your group or organization. For further information, contact:

Triumph Books
542 South Dearborn Street
Suite 750
Chicago, Illinois 60605
(312) 939-3330
Fax (312) 663-3557

CONTRIBUTING WRITER: Mike Babcock

EDITOR: Rob Doster

PHOTO EDITOR: Tim Clark

DESIGN: Anderson Thomas Design
PRODUCTION: Odds & Ends Multimedia

PHOTO CREDITS: Athlon Sports Archive, Nebraska Sports Information, AP/Wide World Photos, Bettmann/Corbis, Time Life Pictures/Getty Images

Printed in U.S.A.

ISBN-13: 978-1-57243-884-2
ISBN-10: 1-57243-884-3

CONTENTS

FOREWORD BY TREV ALBERTS   vii

INTRODUCTION   xi

TRADITIONS AND PAGEANTRY   1

THE GREATEST PLAYERS   29

THE COACHES   63

CORNHUSKER SUPERLATIVES   73

THE RIVALRIES   115

TALKIN' HUSKER FOOTBALL   127

FACTS AND FIGURES   141

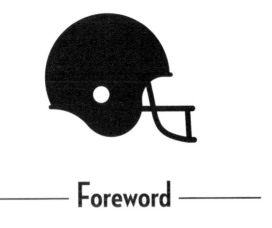

Foreword

There are experiences in life that have a tendency to remain frozen in time. My time at the University of Nebraska was unique in that I seem to be able to recall situations and experiences as if they had just happened. Those memories are forever etched in my heart, and they are a driving force in virtually all that I am today.

Football at Nebraska has earned a reputation for excellence while remaining true to the core values of what makes a Nebraskan. Nebraskans are extremely loyal, hard-working and principled. We expect greatness but not at the expense of our moral core. Having a football team that represented the ideals of the state's citizens was important to our coaches. We were expected to play for four quarters. We never quit. We played as a team, and those who would not play as a team were shunned.

We respected the game and those who came before us and laid the foundation. We were simply there to continue the legacy. We never would have been able to deal with the realization that we were the class that failed to deliver. We played like champions even if the scoreboard failed to reflect it. We were proud to represent the state and its people.

We lost games when I played at Nebraska, but I remember our fans standing and cheering for us in defeat as well as in victory.

Opposing teams were dumbfounded when our fans stood and congratulated them for a good, clean effort, even on those rare occasions when they won. The state is largely defined by the success of its football team. For some, that burden was too heavy. For those of us who persevered, however, it is easy to see why people say, "There is no place like Nebraska."

I will never forget my indoctrination into Husker football as an 18-year-old from Iowa. My family and I drove to Nebraska for a recruiting visit. Entering Lincoln, we turned onto Cornhusker Highway, passed the Big Red Shop and stayed at the Cornhusker Hotel. It was pretty clear that Nebraska football wasn't just a game and not even a passion, but rather a way of life.

I watched as walk-ons from Nebraska gave every ounce of energy in their souls just to earn the right to put on a helmet with a red *N* on the side. I saw teammates cry when they received a Blackshirt and cry again when they had to give it back after being demoted. The first time I learned what it meant to be a Husker was running into Memorial Stadium as a redshirt freshman. It was daunting as 80,000 dressed in red stood in an almost reverential way and saluted their Huskers. I couldn't feel the turf. My knees were weak. I understood this wasn't our team. This wasn't even Coach Osborne's team. This was Nebraska's team!

—Trev Alberts

Introduction

The images are unforgettable and too numerous to count.

The sea of red that engulfs Memorial Stadium on football Saturdays in Lincoln. Johnny Rodgers' magical punt return in the Game of the Century. Bob Devaney, who brought Nebraska's program to the forefront of college football. Tom Osborne, a model of dignity, decorum and commitment on the Nebraska sidelines, amassing wins at an amazing clip. The fabled Blackshirts defense; that unstoppable option offense.

We're distilling the pageantry and drama of Nebraska football into the pages that follow. It's a daunting task. Few college football programs in the country inspire the loyalty and passion that the Cornhusker football program exacts from its fans—and with good reason.

Through the words and images we present, you'll get a taste of what Nebraska football is all about. Decades have passed since players first donned the scarlet and cream, but one thing hasn't changed: Nebraska football is a tradition, a legacy of greatness, a way of life in the Cornhusker State.

TRADITIONS AND PAGEANTRY

The sights and sounds of game day in Lincoln create an unmatched spectacle, a glorious mix of tradition and color and pomp and pageantry. Here's a small sample of what makes Nebraska football unique.

Colors and Nickname

The first football team to represent the University of Nebraska, in 1890, was called the Old Gold Knights. But that nickname was hardly appropriate after the school colors became scarlet and cream in 1892. Prior to 1900, several nicknames were used, among them Bugeaters, Tree-planters, Rattlesnake Boys and Antelopes. Bugeaters is most often applied to those early teams, though it is not clear how common the reference was or even the basis of its use. Several histories associate Bugeaters with the "insect-devouring bullbats" common on the plains. But the nickname also has been associated with a story in an Eastern newspaper about a drought in Nebraska in the 1870s and the hardiness of the state's

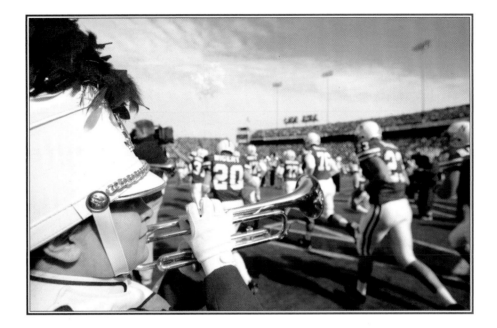

inhabitants, who were credited with a willingness to subsist on bugs rather than be defeated by the elements.

In any case, Charles "Cy" Sherman, a Lincoln newspaper reporter, considered Bugeaters inappropriate and in about 1899 began referring to the university's teams as Cornhuskers. Through Sherman's efforts and those of Albert Watkins Jr., a journalism professor at the university, Cornhuskers became the official nickname in 1900. Sherman, who also was instrumental in establishing the Associated Press national rankings for college football in 1936, was known as "the father of the Cornhuskers" and was made an honorary member of the Nebraska lettermen's club in 1933.

The name of the student yearbook was changed from *Sombrero* to *The Cornhusker* in 1907, and Nebraska officially became "The Cornhusker State" in 1946. Gov. Dwight Griswold presented Sherman with the pen used to sign the bill making the nickname official.

Herbie Husker

Dirk West, an artist in Lubbock, Texas, was commissioned to create Herbie Husker following the 1974 Cotton Bowl. West had drawn the cartoon character on which Herbie was based for the press headquarters at the Cotton Bowl, and Don Bryant, Nebraska's sports information director, had been impressed with it, enough so to initiate the process that produced the now-familiar mascot.

Herbie Husker, who has since been bulked up, was joined by the Lil' Red mascot in 1994. Herbie Husker was chosen as the "Capital One Mascot of the Year" for 2005.

Memorial Stadium

The Cornhuskers have won over 75 percent of the games played at Memorial Stadium, which was dedicated at Homecoming on October 20, 1923, with a scoreless tie with Kansas. Nebraska had spoiled the dedication of the Jayhawks' new Memorial Stadium the previous season, winning 28–0.

The Cornhuskers won their first game at the stadium the week before, however, against Oklahoma 24–0. Work on the concrete and steel stadium, patterned after Ohio State's, hadn't been completed. A crowd estimated at 15,000, some 5,000 fewer than for the dedication game, was on hand.

The completed stadium accommodated 31,000, or a little more than twice what its predecessor, Nebraska Field, held. Nebraska Field ran east and west and was located just to the south of where Memorial Stadium is now. The Cornhuskers had played at Nebraska Field since 1909.

There was talk of replacing Nebraska Field as early as 1915, when Coach E.O. "Jumbo" Stiehm's Cornhuskers went 8–0, including a 20–19 victory against Notre Dame there, and were invited to play in the Rose Bowl game. University officials declined the invitation, however.

Land for the stadium was secured through the efforts of Earl O. Eager, the university's general manager of athletics and a former Cornhusker football player. The diminutive Eager, nicknamed "Dog," was occasionally picked up by teammates and tossed over the goal line, a maneuver that apparently was commonplace before the rules were changed. In any case, a $400,000-plus fund drive for the stadium was initiated in October of 1922, and a ceremonial groundbreaking took place on April 23, 1923.

Bleachers beyond the north and south end zones increased the 31,000 capacity. Success

under coach Bob Devaney led to the first of several Memorial Stadium expansions in 1964, when capacity was increased to 48,000 with the addition of permanent south end zone seats. The center section of the north stadium was added in 1965, increasing the total to 53,000, and the north stands were completed in 1966, bringing capacity to 65,000. Six years later, in the wake of national championships in 1970 and 1971, the south end zone was extended in 1972, increasing the stadium's capacity to 73,650.

Skyboxes and club seating on the west side were added in 1999 and 2000. With the

restructuring required for the club level, seating capacity was at 73,918, a total set to increase to more than 80,000 for 2006 with an addition to the north stadium stands as part of a $50 million expansion project.

Lights were added in 1997 (east side) and 1998 (west side). The first night game at Memorial Stadium, a 34–17 win over Florida State, was played in 1986, with portable lighting.

Despite the expansion on the west side, the original façade has remained intact. The four corners of the stadium include words written for that purpose by Hartley Burr Alexander, a University of Nebraska professor of philosophy at the time. Alexander's words:

Southeast: "In Commendation of the men of Nebraska who served and fell in the Nations Wars."

Southwest: "Not the victory but the action; Not the goal but the game; In the deed the glory."

Northwest: "Courage; Generosity; Fairness; Honor; In these are the true awards of manly sport."

Northeast: "Their Lives they held their countrys trust; They kept its faith; They died its heroes."

Tom Osborne Field

The field at Memorial Stadium was named in honor of coach Tom Osborne following his retirement, which was announced before the 1998 Orange Bowl game and became official on February 4, 1998. The university board of regents waived a waiting period required for such naming of university facilities. Characteristically, Osborne said he would prefer that the field not be named for him.

Tunnel Walk

Among the highlights of Nebraska's game-day experience is the Tunnel Walk, begun in 1994. With the aid of HuskerVision cameras and large video screens, fans have watched the Cornhuskers leave the locker room and walk along a hallway, the tunnel, and through double doors, emerging beneath the south stadium stands and proceeding along a red brick walkway to where they run onto the field at the southwest corner. The walk is conducted to the sounds of the Alan Parsons Project instrumental "Sirius."

With a stadium-expansion project that includes the Tom and Nancy Osborne Athletic Complex, the Cornhusker locker room will move from the south end to the north end, where it was prior to 1973. As a result, the Tunnel Walk also will shift ends of the stadium.

—— The Red Sea ——

When the Cornhuskers play there, Memorial Stadium becomes the third-largest city in the state. Nebraska has a continuing NCAA record of 275 consecutive home sellouts, dating from the Homecoming game against Missouri on November 3, 1962, Bob Devaney's first season as head coach.

With the stadium-expansion project to be completed for the 2006 season, more than 80,000 will fill the stadium on home Saturdays, creating an intimidating, inspiring sea of red. The passion for Nebraska football is such that the 2005 spring intrasquad game drew a crowd of 63,416, breaking a record of 61,417 set the previous spring.

Cornhusker fans have earned a reputation for courtesy toward visiting teams in victory or defeat. After his Florida State team upset No. 3-ranked Nebraska at Memorial Stadium in 1980, Seminoles coach Bobby Bowden praised Cornhusker fans in an open letter published in Lincoln and Omaha newspapers.

When the Cornhuskers score for the first time, fans release hundreds of red and white balloons. They've released plenty of them over the years; Nebraska has not been shut out at home since a 12-0 loss against Kansas State in 1968.

———— Marching Band ————

The Cornhusker band was established in 1879. John Philip Sousa presented the Marching Red a "Distinguished Recognition Trophy" in 1927, and the band received the John Philip Sousa Foundation's Sudler Trophy, recognizing the nation's top university marching band, in 1996. The Marching Red has performed at all of the traditional New Year's Day bowl games and 11 different bowl games total: Rose, Orange, Sugar, Fiesta, Cotton, Citrus, Holiday, Alamo, Sun, Astro-Bluebonnet, Liberty and Independence.

The strains of "Hail Varsity" stir the emotions of Cornhusker fans at every athletic event.

Horseshoe

As players leave the locker room on their way to the field, they tap a lucky horseshoe that has hung above double doors in the hallway opening beneath the south stadium stands and out to the field. No one seems to know where the horseshoe came from. It also hung above double doors when the locker room was in Schulte Fieldhouse at the north end of the stadium. The horseshoe was there for as long as anyone could remember. The north field house, which was razed during construction of the Tom and Nancy Osborne Athletic Complex, opened in 1947. When the new locker room at the north end opens in 2006, presumably the horseshoe will be moved again.

Blackshirts

The Blackshirt tradition began in the mid-1960s, when NCAA rules were changed to allow two-platoon football. Coach Bob Devaney wanted a way to differentiate the first-team defense during practice, and he sent assistant coach Mike Corgan to a local sporting goods store to purchase some pullover contrast jerseys. The story goes that Corgan, who was known for his frugality, bought black pullovers because they weren't selling well and the store owner made him a deal on them.

Initially, the black jerseys were distributed before each day's practice. From the beginning, they were a point of pride, and they came to represent the Cornhusker defense. Now, they are full jerseys, with players' names on the backs and are usually distributed the week of the opening game.

The Blackshirt tradition gained national currency during Charlie McBride's 18-year (1982–1999) tenure as defensive coordinator, with a crossbones logo of its own. Though more than 11 Blackshirts have been distributed at times, only those holding or sharing first-team positions receive them. Some punters also have earned Blackshirts. Despite the exclusivity, "The thing that's good about it is, it entails the whole defense," McBride said. "In general, everybody on the defense is a Blackshirt in some way."

"Dear Old Nebraska U"

There is no place like Nebraska,

Dear old Nebraska U.

Where the girls are the fairest,

The boys are the squarest,

Of any old school that I knew.

There is no place like Nebraska,

Where they're all true blue.

We'll all stick together,

In all kinds of weather,

For Dear old Nebraska U.

"Come A Runnin' Boys"

Come a runnin' boys,

Don't you hear that noise,

Like the thunder in the sky,

How it rolls along,

In a good son,

From the sons of Nebraski.

Now it's coming near,

With a rising cheer,

That will seep all foes away.

So with all our vim, we are bound to win,

And we're going to win today.

For Nebraska and the scarlet

For Nebraska and the cream,

Tho' they go thru many a battle,

Our colors still are seen.

So in contest and in vict'ry

We will wave them for the team,

And 'twill always stir a Cornhusker,

The old scarlet and the cream.

Nebraska's record during Tommie Frazier's four years in Lincoln was 45-4.

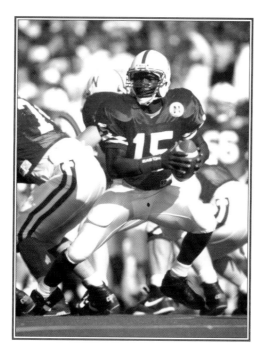

THE GREATEST PLAYERS

Nebraska's roster of greats reads like a who's who of college football legends. The names are familiar to fans of college football, and for the fans of the Huskers' rivals, they still bring a shiver of dread.

The jersey numbers of two Nebraska football players are retired, never to be worn again: Tom Novak's 60 and Bob Brown's 64. There was a time when many more were retired, among them Johnny Rodgers' 20, Dave Rimington's 50 and Rich Glover's 79. But the list was growing to the point that the Cornhuskers were in jeopardy of being short of jersey numbers. So only the two remain retired.

Nebraska has had so many national award winners, so many great players, that they can't all be included here, which is why the following list should be considered representative, not definitive.

TREV ALBERTS
Outside Linebacker, 1990–1993

Alberts, a self-described "average guy" who worked hard, was anything but average. As a senior, he was Nebraska's first Butkus Award winner as the nation's top collegiate linebacker, the Big Eight Defensive Player of the Year, a consensus All-American and a first-team Academic All-American. He also was the Big Eight "Male Athlete of the Year" and an NCAA Top Eight Award winner.

His ability as a pass rusher influenced Tom Osborne's decision to scrap a "50" defense in favor of the 4-3 base alignment that contributed to Nebraska's winning three national championships after Alberts left as the fifth player selected in the 1994 NFL draft, by the Indianapolis Colts.

He holds the Cornhuskers' career record for sacks with 29.5 and shares the single-season record with 15. He also ranks third in career tackles for loss with 45. He went out in style, earning the defensive MVP award in Nebraska's 18–16 loss to Florida State in the 1994 Orange Bowl game.

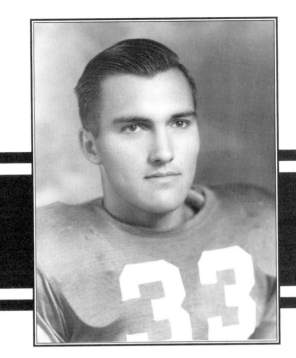

FORREST BEHM
Tackle, 1938–1940

In order to try out for the Cornhusker freshman team, Behm had to buy his own football cleats. He wore size 15, and the equipment manager didn't have any that would fit him. In addition to lacking shoes, Behm lacked impressive credentials. He had played only one varsity season at Lincoln (Nebraska) High School.

In addition, Behm, who had suffered severe burns in a fire as a five-year-old, was awkward. When he ran, he looked like a "cow in mud," according to Henry "Pa" Schulte, who

had been the track-and-field coach and a football assistant at Nebraska until a debilitating disease left him wheelchair-bound.

With Schulte's help and his own shoes, however, Behm not only made the team, but he also excelled, earning All-America recognition as a senior on the 1941 Rose Bowl team. He played tackle alongside guard and linebacker Warren Alfson, who also earned All-America honors that season. Behm, a member of the College Football Hall of Fame, spent 40 years working for Corning International Corp. and in 1965 became president of the company.

BOB BROWN

Guard, 1961–1963

Coach Bob Devaney called Brown "the best two-way player I ever coached." Brown was a unanimous All-American as an offensive guard in 1963, the first African-American at Nebraska to earn All-America recognition. He also was a dominating linebacker, at 6'5" and 260 pounds.

Brown was first-team All–Big Eight twice and a leader on the Cornhuskers' 1963 Big Eight championship team, Nebraska's first conference championship team since 1940. He left Nebraska with a degree and as the second player selected in the 1964 NFL draft. His success continued in the NFL. He was a Pro Bowl selection six times as an offensive tackle and was chosen to the NFL's all-decade team for the 1960s.

The "Boomer" is one of only three former Cornhuskers inducted into the Pro Football Hall of Fame and one of only two also inducted into the College Football Hall of Fame, joining Guy Chamberlin. Roy "Link" Lyman is the third in the Pro Football Hall of Fame.

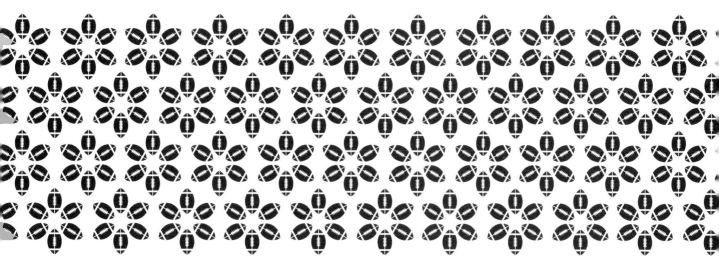

GUY CHAMBERLIN
End, 1913–1915

Lincoln sportswriter "Cy" Sherman described Chamberlin, who came off a farm near Blue Springs, Nebraska, as "the most brilliant player ever developed in the annals of Missouri Valley football." He was 6'2", 200 pounds and fast, running the 100-yard dash in 10 seconds. And most of all, "The Champ" was a winner. He began his college career at Nebraska Wesleyan but was persuaded, after two years there, to transfer to Nebraska. He played on the freshman team in 1913, then became the dominant force on "Jumbo" Stiehm–coached teams that were a combined 15–0–1 in 1914 and 1915.

Chamberlin was chosen as the Most Valuable Player in the Missouri Valley Conference both seasons, playing primarily halfback in 1914 and end in 1915. He returned to halfback for his final game at Nebraska, against rival Iowa, and scored five touchdowns in a 52–7 victory. He earned All-America recognition in 1915 and is a member of both the College and Pro Football Halls of Fame.

ERIC CROUCH
Quarterback, 1998–2001

College football has never had a better option quarterback. Crouch was as good as it gets. When he finished, he was one of only three players in NCAA Division I-A history to rush for 3,000 yards and pass for 4,000 yards during his career. As a senior, he was a cocaptain and joined a select group by rushing for 1,115 yards and passing for 1,510 yards. He finished his career with 59 rushing touchdowns, an NCAA record for a quarterback, and 88 total offensive touchdowns.

He holds 19 school records, including total offense with 7,915 yards, and he won the Heisman Trophy, the Walter Camp Player of the Year award and Davey O'Brien quarterback award in 2001, when he carried the Cornhuskers to the BCS national championship game in the Rose Bowl.

His Heisman Trophy season was highlighted by a 95-yard touchdown run against Missouri and a touchdown reception on a 63-yard pass play against Oklahoma.

"I really don't care about any personal honors.
*That's just kind of how I've been. If I receive the Heisman Trophy, I'm going to give it to the team. That's just the kind of player I am, the person I am." —*ERIC CROUCH A MONTH BEFORE HE WON THE HEISMAN TROPHY

SAM FRANCIS
Fullback, 1934–1936

Legendary Kansas basketball coach "Phog" Allen recruited Francis, and the talented multi-sport athlete from Oberlin, Kansas, nearly became a Jayhawk. He even moved into a dorm at Kansas before changing his mind, with some persuasion from Nebraska track-and-field coach "Pa" Schulte.

Francis was a world-class shot putter, finishing fourth at the Olympic Games in 1936, prior to his senior football season. He and Lloyd Cardwell made Coach D.X. Bible's single-wing offense click. During their three seasons, the Cornhuskers were a combined 19–7–1, including 7–2 in 1936, the first season for the Associated Press national rankings. Nebraska finished ninth in the final poll.

Francis was runner-up to Yale's Larry Kelley in close voting for the Heisman Trophy in 1936, when he earned All-America honors. He was the first player selected in the 1937 NFL draft, but his professional football career was brief and undistinguished. He is among 12 former Nebraska players in the College Football Hall of Fame.

TOMMIE FRAZIER
Quarterback, 1992–1995

Had it been up to him, Frazier wouldn't have made a recruiting visit to Nebraska, much less accepted the Cornhuskers' scholarship offer. Nebraska was the last of his five scheduled visits, and he was weary of the process. But he had given his word, his mom told him, and he was going to go. Husker fans are forever grateful.

Frazier was at his best when the stakes were highest. He became the starter in the sixth game of his freshman season and relinquished the job only because of blood-clot problems, which sidelined him for seven games as a junior. But he returned to play in the 1995 Orange Bowl game, directing the Cornhuskers to two fourth-quarter touchdowns in a 24–17 victory over Miami that gave coach Tom Osborne his first national title. Frazier was the offensive MVP in that game as well as in the 1996 Fiesta Bowl, where he rushed for 199 yards and two touchdowns as Nebraska overwhelmed Florida 62–24 to win another national championship and claim a place among the greatest teams in history.

Frazier won the Johnny Unitas Award as a senior and finished second in voting for the Heisman Trophy. His career record as a starter was 33–3. He is now the head coach at Doane College in Crete, Nebraska.

"*I had the approach* that one day Nebraska would have a black quarterback, so why not me? I wasn't saying it would be me, just that it could be." —TURNER GILL

TURNER GILL
Quarterback, 1981–1983

Gill set the standard by which Cornhusker quarterbacks are measured. Though he was recruited as an option quarterback, and considered himself a runner, he could have been a drop-back passer. He completed 54 percent of his passes, with 34 touchdowns and only 11 interceptions. He threw 125 passes in a row without an interception at one point during his career. He also rushed for 1,317 yards.

Nebraska won a spirited recruiting battle with Oklahoma for Gill, who came from Fort Worth, Texas. He was part of a talented trio that Sooner coach Barry Switzer nicknamed the "Triplets." The other two-thirds of the "Triplets" were I-back Mike Rozier and wingback Irving Fryar. They played together for three seasons, during which Nebraska went 33–5 and could have won a national championship or two—or even three. They never lost to Oklahoma.

Gill's record as a starter was 28–2, including 20–0 in the Big Eight. He was a three-time, first-team all-conference selection and finished fourth in voting for the Heisman Trophy in 1983, when Rozier won the award. Gill also played baseball at Nebraska, as well as professionally.

He is in his first year as head coach at the University of Buffalo.

RICH GLOVER
Middle Guard, 1970–1972

The zenith of Glover's career was the 1971 Game of the Century at Oklahoma. He was matched against the Sooners' All-America center, Tom Brahaney, and responded with what was at the time a school-record 22 tackles. Oklahoma had no answer for his strength and quickness. Teammate Johnny Rodgers said, "Nobody earned their All-America status playing against Richie Glover."

Glover was a two-time consensus All-American and won both the Outland Trophy and the Lombardi Award as a senior. He fin-ished third in voting for the Heisman Trophy, won by Rodgers, in 1972.

Coach Bob Devaney said if it had been up to him to pick the Heisman Trophy winner that season, he would have had to flip a coin between those two. Glover was credited with 100 tackles, including nine for losses, in 1972 as the Cornhuskers ranked in the top 10 nationally in total defense, scoring defense and pass defense. He is a member of the College Football Hall of Fame.

LARRY JACOBSON
Defensive Tackle, 1969–1971

When defensive line coach Monte Kiffin called to tell Jacobson that he had won the Outland Trophy, Jacobson asked what the Outland Trophy was. He even asked Kiffin to spell it for him. That he would receive an award as the nation's top collegiate lineman was a shock to Jacobson, who hadn't even earned all-conference honorable mention the previous season as a junior.

Surprise or not, the 6'6", 250-pound Jacobson was Nebraska's first major award winner and the first of seven Cornhuskers who have won the Outland Trophy (Dave Rimington won it twice). "Big Jake" also won the Knute Rockne Award in 1971, as well as earning first-team All-America and Academic All-America recognition. And he was a finalist for the Lombardi Award.

Jacobson was one of three Cornhuskers selected in the first round of the 1972 NFL draft—the others were Jeff Kinney and Jerry Tagge—and he played four professional seasons.

WAYNE MEYLAN
Middle Guard, 1965–1967

The square-jawed Meylan began his career as an offensive guard but moved to defense before the third game of his sophomore season and immediately became a dominating force with his strength and quickness. As a junior, he blocked three punts and recovered two of them for touchdowns.

Meylan was a consensus All-American twice and the UPI Defensive Lineman of the Year in 1967, when the Cornhuskers led the nation in total defense and pass defense and ranked third in scoring defense. They shut out four opponents, including three in a row. He was credited with 119 tackles, a school record at the time, and finished ninth in voting for the Heisman Trophy.

He was successful in business and had a passion for flying World War II planes at air shows. He died in a plane crash at an air show in his home state of Michigan. He was 41 years old.

He is a member of the College Football Hall of Fame.

TOM NOVAK
Center-Linebacker, 1946–1949

In the four seasons Novak played, Nebraska's record was a combined 11–26, under three different coaches. But wins and losses didn't define Novak, who played center, fullback and linebacker with a fierce determination reflected by his nickname, "Trainwreck."

Lincoln Star sports editor Norris Anderson wrote that Novak was "a beacon in the dark years. No man ever gave more to Cornhusker football." He was a first-team all-conference pick four times, the only Cornhusker ever to be so honored. And he earned All-America recognition in 1949.

Lyell Bremser, a broadcasting legend as the voice of the Cornhuskers, paid tribute to Novak when he finished at Nebraska. "My eyes have never seen Tom Novak's equal at any position," Bremser said. "As football players go, the good Lord made Tom Novak and threw away the mold."

The lettermen's club retired his No. 60 jersey immediately after his senior season, and the Tom Novak Award was established in his honor in 1950. The award is presented annually to the Cornhusker senior who "best exemplifies courage and determination despite all odds in the manner of Nebraska All-America center Tom Novak."

BOBBY REYNOLDS
Halfback, 1950–1952

His sophomore season defined the 5'11", 180-pound Reynolds. He led the nation in scoring with 157 points, on 22 touchdowns and 25 extra points. Eighteen of his touchdowns came on runs of 11 yards or more. He was an All-American and finished fifth in voting for the Heisman Trophy—as a sophomore, remember. He became "Mr. Touchdown," a nickname *Collier's* magazine made national.

Reynolds rushed for 1,342 yards in nine games in 1950, a school record that would hold for 32 years. He was never able to duplicate that success, however, because of injuries, beginning with a separated shoulder suffered during coach Bill Glassford's grueling preseason training camp at the university's agricultural college in Curtis, Nebraska—known as "Camp Curtis."

Another shoulder separation and a burned cornea from the lime used to mark the field were among the other injuries that limited Reynolds to 13 games in his final two seasons. Even so, he was a team captain in 1952. On his death, at age 54, the *Lincoln Journal* described him as the "transcendent football hero."

DAVE RIMINGTON
Center, 1979–1982

Rimington came from Omaha (Nebraska) South High School to become one of the most decorated offensive linemen in college football history. He earned back-to-back Outland Trophies, the only player ever to do so, as well as the Lombardi Award in 1982, when he was a Cornhusker cocaptain. He also finished fifth in the Heisman Trophy voting. He was a two-time All-American, a two-time Academic All-American and first-team All–Big Eight three times. As a junior he was chosen as the Big Eight "Offensive Player of the Year," the only interior lineman ever to be so honored. Rimington was a first-round NFL draft choice and played seven professional seasons. A member of the College Football Hall of Fame and the Academic All-American Hall of Fame, he is the president of the Boomer Esiason Foundation, which sponsors the Rimington Award, presented to the nation's top collegiate center. Former Cornhusker Dominic Raiola received the first Rimington Award in 2000.

> ## "I probably should have made a fair catch."
>
> —JOHNNY RODGERS ON HIS 72-YARD PUNT RETURN FOR A TOUCHDOWN IN THE
> 1971 GAME OF THE CENTURY

JOHNNY RODGERS
Wingback, 1970–1972

"The Jet" finished his career in style, rushing for three touchdowns, catching a touchdown pass and throwing a touchdown pass in the Cornhuskers' 40–6 victory against Notre Dame in the 1973 Orange Bowl game. He lined up at I-back in that game, a surprise to the Fighting Irish.

Rodgers envisioned playing tailback at Southern California when he came out of Omaha (Nebraska) Technical High School. But the Trojans weren't interested, so he stayed in the state and became the top pass receiver and kick returner in Big Eight history, setting 41 school records and four NCAA records for Cornhusker teams that were a combined 32–2–2 and won two national championships.

The 1971 team, still regarded by some as the greatest in college football history, wouldn't have gone 13–0 without Rodgers' kick returns, according to Tom Osborne, his position coach. Rodgers' most famous punt return was a 72-yarder to begin the scoring in the 1971 Game of the Century at Oklahoma.

He was a three-time all-conference selection and won the Heisman Trophy and Walter Camp Player of the Year award in 1972. He is a member of the College Football Hall of Fame.

"Johnny Rodgers probably

could impact a football game in more ways

than anyone I've been involved with."

—Tom Osborne

"Roger [Craig] and I *are pretty good friends. If he wasn't really a top running back, I might be upset. I wouldn't show it, of course, but it might bother me. But Roger does the job, so what more can you ask?"* —ROZIER ON ALTERNATING AT I-BACK WITH CRAIG

MIKE ROZIER
I-back, 1981–1983

Because of an air traffic controllers' strike, Rozier had to take a bus from Camden, New Jersey, to Lincoln before his sophomore season. The trip took a day and a half. He played his freshman season at Coffeyville (Kansas) Community College, rushing for 1,100 yards in a Wishbone offense. And he missed two games.

He shared time with Roger Craig his first season at Nebraska and then broke the school rushing record as a junior, gaining 1,689 yards and finishing 10th in voting for the Heisman Trophy. Craig moved to fullback in 1982 and was plagued by injuries. The rushing record lasted less than a year.

Rozier shattered it as a senior, rushing for 2,148 yards—becoming the second player in NCAA history to run for at least 2,000—and 29 touchdowns. He ran for 929 yards in the final four games. He earned All-America recognition for a second consecutive season in 1983 and also won the Heisman Trophy, the Maxwell Award and the Walter Camp Player of the Year award. He holds the career rushing record at Nebraska, 4,780 yards, and averaged an NCAA-record 7.16 yards per carry for his career.

GEORGE SAUER
Fullback, 1931–1933

Coach D.X. Bible called Sauer "probably my best all-around athlete." He earned letters in four sports and became a starter on the football team in the second game of his sophomore season, never relinquishing the job. He earned first-team All–Big Six honors three times and All-America recognition as a senior.

The Cornhuskers lost only four games in Sauer's three seasons. They were 8–1 in 1933, their only loss coming at perennial power Pittsburgh, 6–0. Nebraska shut out six opponents. Sauer kicked a field goal against Oklahoma that season, even though he had never kicked in competition to that point.

In addition to his athletic skills, Sauer was a "thoroughly decent guy," according to legendary New York City sportswriter Red Smith. He scored both touchdowns in the West's 12–0 Shrine Game victory following his senior season and went on to a coaching career that included stints at New Hampshire, Kansas, the Naval Academy and Baylor. He is a member of the College Football Hall of Fame.

WILL SHIELDS
Offensive Guard, 1989–1992

True freshmen rarely played in the offensive line under coach Tom Osborne. Jake Young was the first in the modern era, playing in 1986. The soft-spoken Shields was the second, three seasons later. He also was the Cornhuskers' second scholarship recruit out of Oklahoma, coming from Lawton.

Shields was the first Nebraska lineman since Dave Rimington to earn first-team all-conference recognition as a sophomore. He would earn it twice more and be awarded the Outland Trophy as a senior, the fifth Cornhusker to be so honored. He also was a semifinalist for the Lombardi Award.

He was the last Cornhusker guard to carry the ball on Osborne's "fumbleroosky" play before the NCAA changed its rules following the 1992 season. He gained 16 yards on the play against Colorado.

A third-round draft pick of the Kansas City Chiefs, Shields has been selected for 11 consecutive Pro Bowls and has started more than 200 consecutive games. He was the NFL "Man of the Year" in 2003 for his charitable endeavors and contributions to the community.

DEAN STEINKUHLER
Offensive Guard, 1981–1983

At Nebraska's "Double Hundred Celebration" honoring coaches Bob Devaney and Tom Osborne in 1983, comedian Bob Hope said the 6'3", 270-pound Steinkuhler should wear a license plate instead of a number on his jersey. He was a big guy from a small town, the smallest town to produce a consensus All-America football player in the post–World War II era. The population of Burr, Nebraska, was 110.

Steinkuhler played eight-man football as a senior at nearby Sterling High School and didn't earn all-conference recognition at his primary position, fullback. As a senior at Nebraska, however, in addition to earning All-America honors, he won both the Outland Trophy and Lombardi Award. Dave Rimington had won both awards the previous season, giving the Cornhuskers an unprecedented three consecutive Outland Trophies (Rimington won two) and two consecutive Lombardi Awards.

Steinkuhler anchored the line for Nebraska's "Scoring Explosion" offense in 1983. He was the second player picked in the 1984 NFL draft, behind teammate Irving Fryar, a wingback. It was only the second time in history that the top two picks had come from the same school.

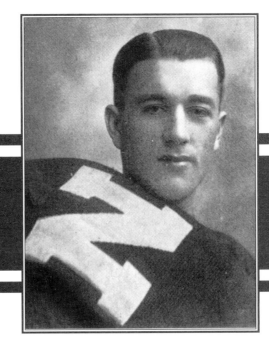

CLARENCE SWANSON
End, 1918–1921

Swanson was captain of Coach Fred Dawson's first Cornhusker team in 1921. He was "a natural leader of men" according to the student yearbook, *The Cornhusker*. As such, he was "bound to be successful as captain," it predicted. He was, and so was the team.

Nebraska was the Missouri Valley Conference champion, winning seven of eight games by a combined score of 283–17. The Cornhuskers' only loss was at Notre Dame, 7–0. They defeated powerful Pittsburgh 10–0, with Swanson scoring the touchdown on a 69-yard pass play. He was prominent on Pittsburgh's all-opponent team and was a first-team all-conference selection.

His great-grandson, Barrett Ruud, is Nebraska's all-time tackles leader. The Canton Bulldogs tried to sign Swanson to a professional contract, but he opted to go into business in Lincoln. Later, he served as president of the university's board of regents and in that capacity was involved in bringing Bob Devaney from Wyoming to Lincoln. He is a member of the College Football Hall of Fame.

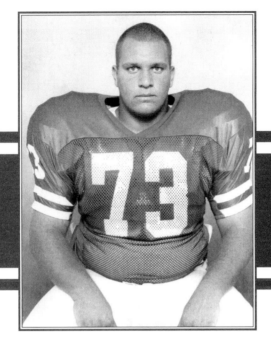

AARON TAYLOR
Guard-Center, 1994–1997

Had things worked out as Taylor wanted, he would have played at a school in Texas. Though he spent his pre–high school years on military bases in Germany, he went to high school in Wichita Falls, Texas. But because of his height, 6'1", no Texas school was interested enough to offer a scholarship.

Nebraska's option offense needed big, aggressive linemen who could move. Height was a secondary consideration. So Taylor picked the Cornhuskers and justified their faith in his abilities. He became the only Husker to be named an All-American at two different positions, earning the honor at center as a junior and at guard as a senior, when he won the Outland Trophy. Center wasn't his natural position, according to offensive line coach Milt Tenopir, but he agreed to move following the graduation of All-American Aaron Graham.

Taylor played on three national championship teams, two as a starter. He was a three-time first-team all-conference selection and a cocaptain as a senior, when he set a school record for knockdown blocks, or "pancakes," with 137.

ED WEIR
Tackle, 1923–1925

Notre Dame's Knute Rockne called Weir, who
came from Superior, Nebraska, the best tackle
he had ever seen, and with good reason. Weir's
Cornhusker teams defeated Notre Dame in
1923 and again in 1925. And those were Notre
Dame's only losses those seasons. The Irish
defeated Nebraska 34–6 at South Bend in 1924,
and afterward, Rockne went to the Cornhusker
locker room to shake Weir's hand.

Weir was most dominant on defense. He
was among the first to use a "red-dogging"
tactic, setting up about a yard off the line of
scrimmage and attacking at the snap. But he
also ran with the ball, caught passes, punted
and kicked placements. His defensive play
helped frustrate Illinois' Red Grange, who finished with negative yardage in a 14–0 loss
against Nebraska in 1925.

Weir was the Cornhuskers' captain as a
junior and senior, and he earned All-America
honors both seasons. He is a member of the
College Football Hall of Fame.

ZACH WIEGERT
Offensive Tackle, 1991–1994

In 1994, Wiegert, a three-time first-team All–Big Eight selection from Fremont, Nebraska, joined fellow All-American Brenden Stai in what coach Tom Osborne described as possibly the best right-side tackle-guard combination in Cornhusker history. The 6'5", 300-pound Wiegert was the Outland Trophy winner and the UPI national lineman of the year, and he finished ninth in voting for the Heisman Trophy. Oh yes, and he was a cocaptain on Osborne's first national championship team, which finished 13–0.

Wiegert started 36 consecutive games and allowed only one sack. He earned a perfect 2.0 grade in a 45–17 victory against Kansas in 1994. "That maybe has happened sometime before in my 33 years here," Osborne said. "But I can't remember anybody playing 65 or 70 plays and having a perfect grade at that level." Wiegert's performance was "one of the finest we've ever had an offensive lineman have."

GRANT WISTROM
Rush End, 1994–1997

Wistrom considered leaving Nebraska for the NFL as a junior. But he returned and was an inspirational leader on a third national championship team in his four seasons. He and tackle Jason Peter drove the defense as cocaptains in 1997, with their attitude as well as their relentless play.

Wistrom was a two-time consensus All-American as well as a two-time, first-team Academic All-American, the second Cornhusker to achieve that double-double; Dave Rimington was the first. Wistrom also was a two-time Big 12 Defensive Player of the Year. He won the Lombardi Award as a senior, as well as the NCAA Top Eight Award. He was outstanding on and off the field.

He still holds the school career record for tackles for loss with 58.5. He was the sixth player selected in the 1998 NFL draft. "I've been around and seen a lot of good ones, and I'll guarantee you, Grant is one of the best," longtime Cornhusker defensive coordinator Charlie McBride said.

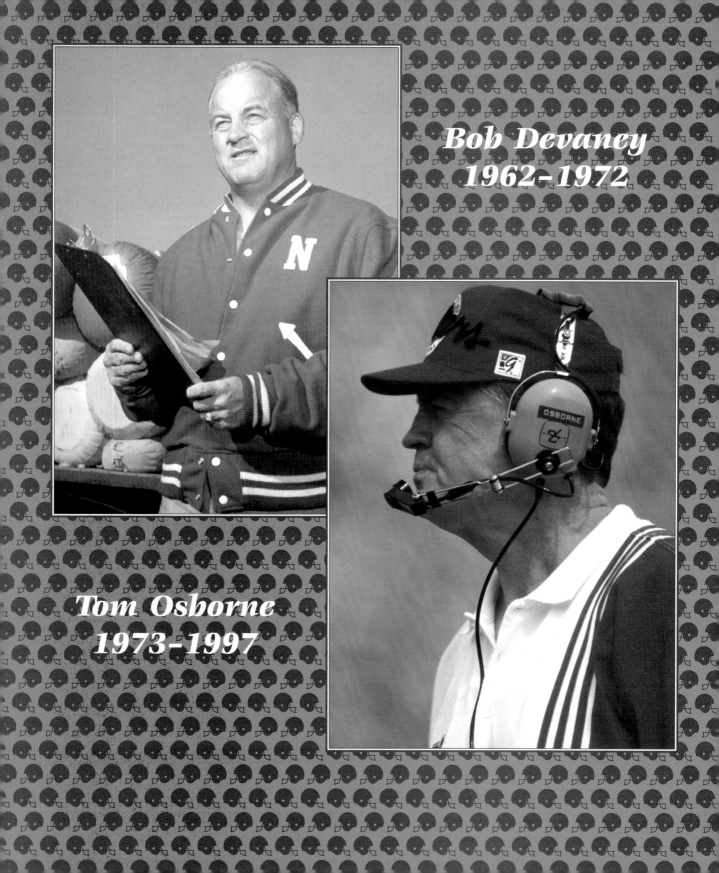

Bob Devaney
1962–1972

Tom Osborne
1973–1997

THE COACHES

The roots of Nebraska's football tradition run deep, as evidenced by an attempt to lure Knute Rockne away from Notre Dame after Ernie Bearg resigned as head coach following the 1928 season.

Bearg's four teams were a combined 23-7-3, with a Big Six title in his final season. But his use of deception rather than a more physical approach on offense drew fan criticism and led to his resignation. Rockne wasn't interested in the job but suggested that D.X. Bible might be.

Bible was interested enough to leave Texas A&M and become the Cornhuskers' coach from 1929 to 1936. During those eight seasons his teams were a combined 50-15-7 with six conference championships. Bible, also Nebraska's athletic director beginning in 1932, would leave for Texas and recommend Oklahoma coach Lawrence McCeney "Biff" Jones as a replacement.

Bible and Jones are among six coaches in the College Football Hall of Fame who spent time at Nebraska. Two of the other four coached the Cornhuskers only briefly. E.N. Robinson, whose claim to fame came at Brown (where he was a multi-sport athlete), began his coaching career at Nebraska in 1896 and 1897. He was succeeded by Fielding Yost, who spent the 1898 season there before moving on.

The most familiar of the Cornhuskers' Hall of Fame coaches, of course, are Bob Devaney and Tom Osborne, the first major college coaches to reach 100 or more victories in consecutive careers at the same school, though neither has the best winning percentage among Nebraska's coaches. That distinction belongs to E.O. "Jumbo" Stiehm, whose "Stiehmrollers" were 35-2-3 (.913) from 1911 to 1915.

——— Bob Devaney ———
1962-1972

As it had done some 30 years earlier, Nebraska gauged the interest of a nationally known coach to fill a vacancy after Bill Jennings was fired following a 3–6–1 season in 1961—Michigan State's Duffy Daugherty. University of Nebraska Chancellor Clifford Hardin, who had been an agriculture professor at Michigan State, encouraged the contact. Daugherty said thanks but no thanks.

He also said the Cornhuskers should consider hiring Devaney, a former assistant who had coached Wyoming to a record of 35–10–5 in five seasons. Devaney wasn't Nebraska Athletic Director "Tippy" Dye's first choice. But the pugnacious Irishman from Saginaw, Michigan, proved to be the man for the job,

instantly turning the Cornhuskers into winners with players Jennings had recruited.

Under Devaney's direction, Nebraska won eight conference championships, including seven outright, and two national championships, back-to-back. Devaney, who became athletic director in 1967, had planned to step aside as coach after the second national title in 1971. But he was persuaded to remain another season in an attempt to coach the Cornhuskers to an unprecedented third consecutive national title. Though Nebraska came up short in 1972, his final three teams were a combined 33–2–2.

Like his coaching mentor Daugherty, Devaney was a storyteller, and his blue-collar

"To me, after seeing how Biggie [Munn] and Duffy [Daugherty] *operated, it was obvious that the big key to getting things done was to have a great group of assistants. I think the biggest mistake I made when I first went to Wyoming was trying to do all the coaching myself." —*Bob Devaney in his **1981** Autobiography

background enabled him to empathize with many of those he recruited.

His immediate success—the Cornhuskers went 9–2 in his first season—raised expectations to such a degree that after 6–4 records in 1967 and 1968, boosters in Omaha circulated a petition calling for his ouster. He weathered the storm, however, and set about restructuring his offense, with the primary responsibility given to a young assistant, receivers coach Tom Osborne.

Osborne, who called the plays from the coaches' box during the national championship seasons, was Devaney's handpicked successor, a decision made and announced prior to the 1972 season.

BOB DEVANEY
YEAR-BY-YEAR AT NEBRASKA

YEAR	RECORD	BOWL GAME
1962	9–2	Gotham
1963	10–1	Orange
1964	9–2	Cotton
1965	10–1	Orange
1966	9–2	Sugar
1967	6–4	—
1968	6–4	—
1969	9–2	Sun
1970	11–0–1	Orange (National Champions)
1971	13–0	Orange (National Champions)
1972	9–2–1	Orange

Tom Osborne
1973-1997

When he succeeded Devaney, Osborne didn't imagine he would spend 25 years as Nebraska's head coach. He figured the best-case scenario was maybe five years.

"Bob always had a built-in grace factor because he turned the program around," Osborne has said. "I wasn't going to have that opportunity because I was more of a caretaker."

Osborne was a native son, a Nebraskan who had been a multi-sport athlete at both Hastings (Nebraska) High and Hastings College. He hadn't planned to pursue coaching. Rather, it was going to be a means to an end.

After a brief professional football career, he sought a job on Devaney's first staff at Nebraska while working on a post-graduate degree. Devaney offered room and board, and he accepted.

After earning a doctorate in educational psychology, however, Osborne chose coaching over the classroom, a choice that produced remarkable results. Every one of his teams won at least nine games and played in bowl games. The 25 consecutive bowl trips made by his teams are an NCAA record for a coach; Bear Bryant is second with 24. And Osborne coached the Cornhuskers to three national

"He goes out fishing and he's competing against himself and the fish. Of course, I'm going to see things from a biased point of view. But to me, it's excellence, excellence in fishing, excellence in whatever he does. More than beating somebody, it's just that he enjoys the journey to excellence. He has said many times, and it's absolutely true from my perception, that it's been the process of a season or the process of the road to a championship from which he gets his most satisfaction." —WIFE NANCY OSBORNE

championships in his final four seasons, compiling a record of 60–3 in his final five seasons, all with 11 or more victories.

His teams won or shared 13 conference titles, and his winning percentage of .836 (255–49–3) was the nation's best among active coaches before he retired. His percentage ranked fifth all time in Division I.

Osborne emphasized the journey rather than the destination, and his philosophy was expressed in the title of an autobiographical book he wrote, *More Than Winning*. He stepped aside after the third national championship—becoming the first coach ever to retire after winning a national title—for health and personal reasons. The field at Memorial Stadium is named in his honor. And he was inducted into the College Football Hall of Fame in 1998, after the Hall's three-year waiting period was waived.

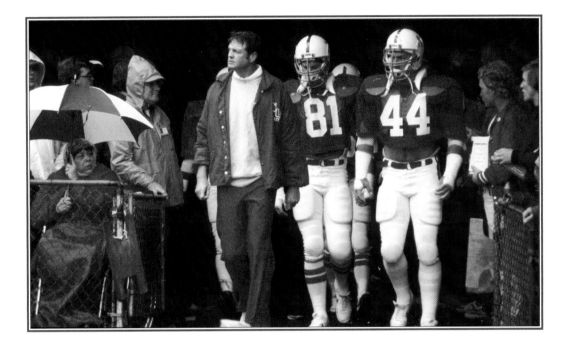

TOM OSBORNE
YEAR-BY-YEAR AT NEBRASKA

YEAR	RECORD	BOWL GAME
1973	9–2–1	Cotton
1974	9–3	Sugar
1975	10–2	Fiesta
1976	9–3–1	Astro-Bluebonnet
1977	9–3	Liberty
1978	9–3	Orange
1979	10–2	Cotton
1980	10–2	Sun
1981	9–3	Orange

YEAR	RECORD	BOWL GAME
1982	12–1	Orange
1983	12–1	Orange
1984	10–2	Sugar
1985	9–3	Fiesta
1986	10–2	Sugar
1987	10–2	Fiesta
1988	11–2	Orange
1989	10–2	Fiesta
1990	9–3	Citrus
1991	9–2–1	Orange
1992	9–3	Orange
1993	11–1	Orange
1994	13–0	Orange (National Champions)
1995	12–0	Fiesta (National Champions)
1996	11–2	Orange
1997	13–0	Orange (National Champions)

"As I said many times, to the chagrin of many Nebraska fans, I'm not in it to win the national championship." —TOM OSBORNE BEFORE THE OKLAHOMA GAME IN 1994

CORNHUSKER SUPERLATIVES

Nebraska football history is littered with moments of greatness—National Championships won, great games played, superior individual efforts, memorable upsets and more. Here is a small sample of that record of achievement.

The Championships

NATIONAL CHAMPIONSHIPS 1970 (AP)

Everything fell into place for Coach Bob Devaney's Cornhuskers on New Year's Day. No. 1 Texas, the UPI national champion, lost to Notre Dame in the Cotton Bowl, 24–11. And No. 2 Ohio State was upset by Stanford in the Rose Bowl, 27–17, leaving the top spot in the Associated Press poll open.

Nebraska, which was No. 3 in both polls going into the Orange Bowl game against No. 5 Louisiana State, was aware of the upsets before the kickoff in Miami. And the Cornhuskers' 17–12 victory was sufficient for Nebraska's first national championship, despite lobbying by Notre Dame.

Coach Ara Parseghian argued that since his Fighting Irish had upset the No. 1 team, they should move from fourth to first, despite a late-season loss against USC—with whom Nebraska had tied. However, "the writers knew who was best," Devaney said after the final AP rankings were released.

The Cornhuskers, whose only blemish was the 21–21 tie in the second game of the season at Los Angeles, were an overwhelming pick by the AP voters.

Linebacker Jerry Murtaugh and offensive tackle Bob Newton earned All-America recognition on a team that included six other players who would be so honored during their careers.

Bob Devaney with Oklahoma coach Chuck Fairbanks, prior to 1971's Game of the Century.

1971 (AP, UPI)

Devaney's next-to-last team was regarded by many as the best in college football history at the time, a claim that was difficult to refute. The Big Eight Conference produced the top three teams in the final AP rankings. The Cornhuskers were followed by Oklahoma and Colorado, a finish unequaled beforeor since.

The national title was determined on Thanksgiving Day at Norman, Oklahoma, when No. 1 Nebraska defeated the No. 2 Sooners 35–31 in what was described as the Game of the Century.

The Cornhuskers would defeat another No. 2–ranked opponent in the Orange Bowl game, overwhelming Alabama and coach Bear Bryant 38–6.

Nebraska had an impressive offense, led by wingback Johnny Rodgers, quarterback Jerry Tagge and I-back Jeff Kinney, all of whom earned All-America honors. But the Blackshirts, who included seven first-team all-conference players, made the difference. Nebraska ranked

THE 1971 NEBRASKA CORNHUSKERS

IS THIS HISTORY'S GREATEST TEAM? JUDGE FOR YOURSELF:

September 11	Nebraska 34, Oregon 7
September 18	Nebraska 35, Minnesota 7
September 25	Nebraska 34, Texas A&M 7
October 2	Nebraska 42, Utah State 6
October 9	Nebraska 36, Missouri 0
October 16	Nebraska 55, Kansas 0
October 23	Nebraska 41, Oklahoma State 13
October 30	Nebraska 31, #9 Colorado 7
November 6	Nebraska 37, Iowa State 0
November 13	Nebraska 44, Kansas State 17
November 25	Nebraska 35, #2 Oklahoma 31
December 4	Nebraska 45, Hawaii 3
January 1	Nebraska 38, #2 Alabama 6

second in the nation in rushing defense, third in scoring defense and fifth in total defense, with three defensive All-Americans: middle guard Rich Glover, end Willie Harper and tackle Larry Jacobson, who won Nebraska's first Outland Trophy.

A year later Glover would win both the Outland Trophy and the Lombardi Award, and Rodgers would become the Cornhuskers' first Heisman Trophy winner. But Nebraska, which went into the 1972 season with a 32-game unbeaten streak and 23-game winning streak, would come up short of a third consecutive national championship, something no program has ever done.

The 1994 Cornhuskers

1994 (AP, COACHES)

Nebraska had to overcome adversity to provide coach Tom Osborne with his first national championship. First, the Cornhuskers lost safety Mike Minter to a season-ending knee injury in the second game at Texas Tech. Then they lost quarterback Tommie Frazier to a blood-clot problem after the fourth game. And, if that weren't enough, they briefly lost Frazier's replacement, Brook Berringer, to a collapsed lung, which led to sophomore walk-on Matt Turman's starting at Kansas State.

But Berringer was 7–0 as a starter and led the team to the Big Eight championship and an Orange Bowl match-up with No. 3–ranked Miami—on the Hurricanes' home field. He passed for 1,295 yards and 10 touchdowns, playing the equivalent of only eight full games.

Frazier returned to action and started the Orange Bowl game. But Berringer also contributed to the 24–17 comeback victory on New Year's night, after which the 13–0 Cornhuskers were voted No. 1 in both polls, despite the fact that Penn State had finished 12–0 and was hoping for a split vote.

Nebraska was led by three All-Americans: linebacker Ed Stewart, offensive guard Brenden Stai and offensive tackle Zach Wiegert, who also won the Outland Trophy. Sophomore I-back Lawrence Phillips rushed for 1,722 yards and finished eighth in voting for the Heisman Trophy.

The Cornhuskers had vowed to return to the Orange Bowl to win a national championship after losing there the previous season to a heavily favored Florida State team, 18–16, when Byron Bennett's 45-yard field-goal attempt sailed wide left on the final play of the game.

Reggie Baul

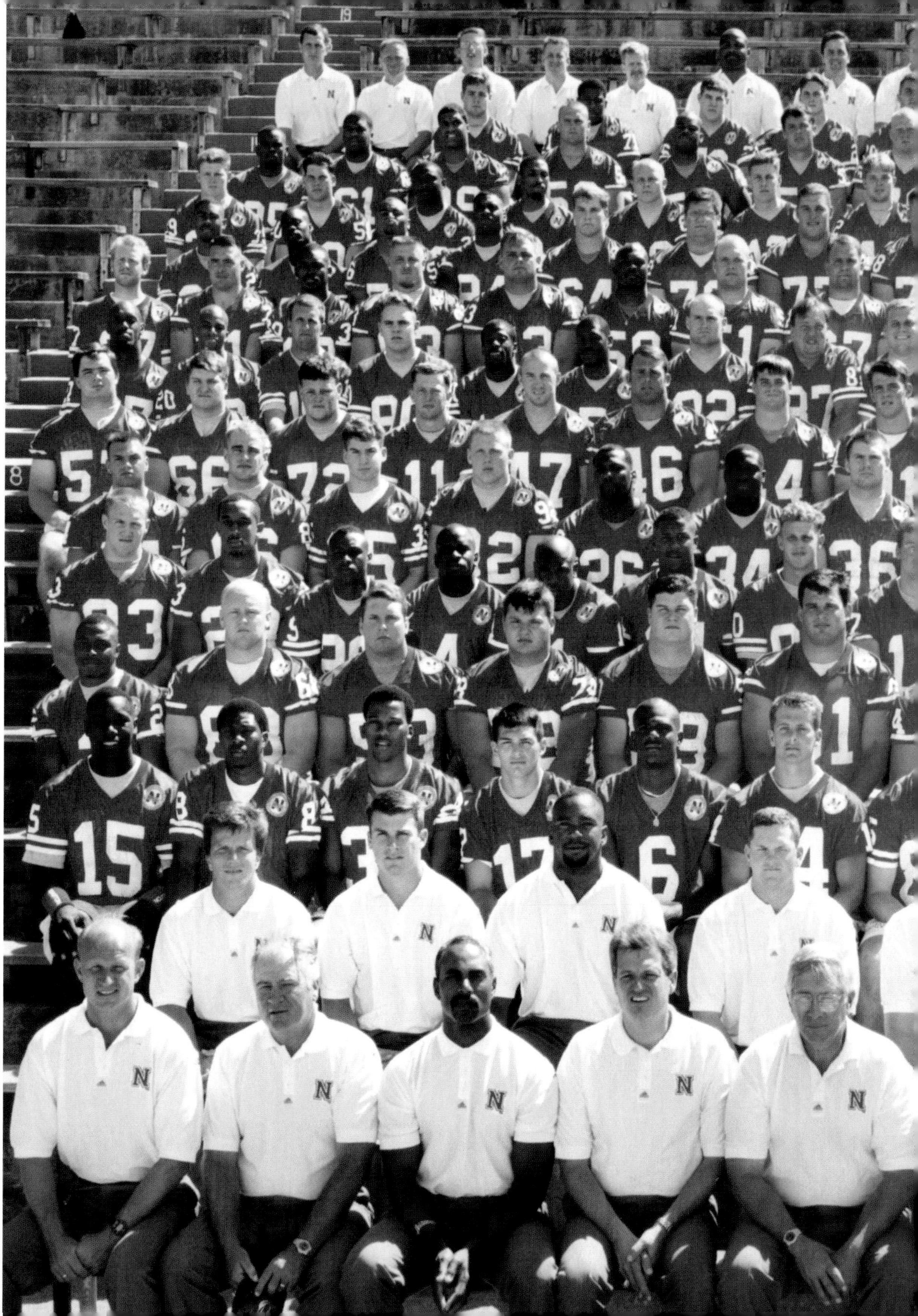

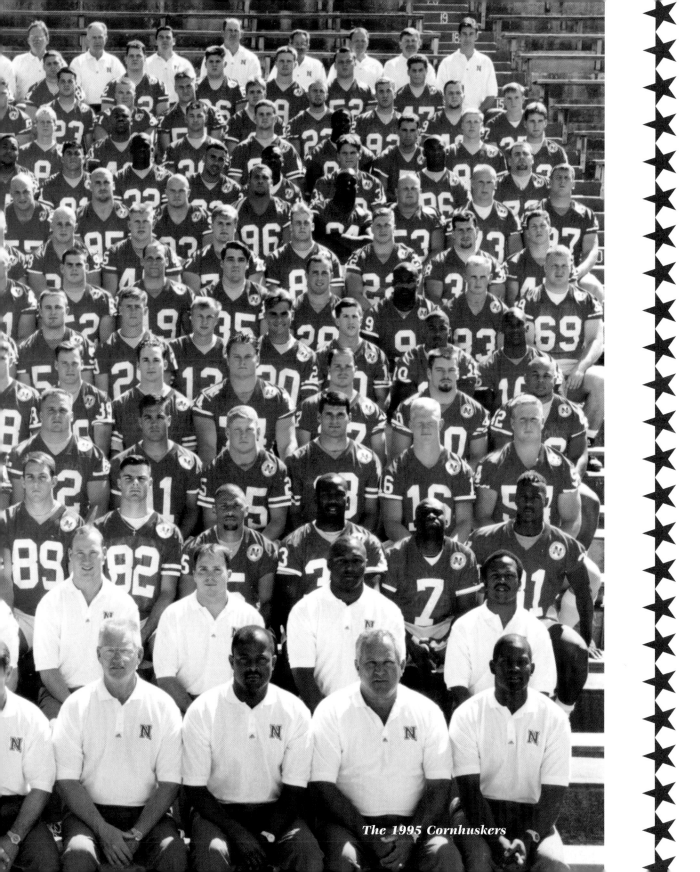

The 1995 Cornhuskers

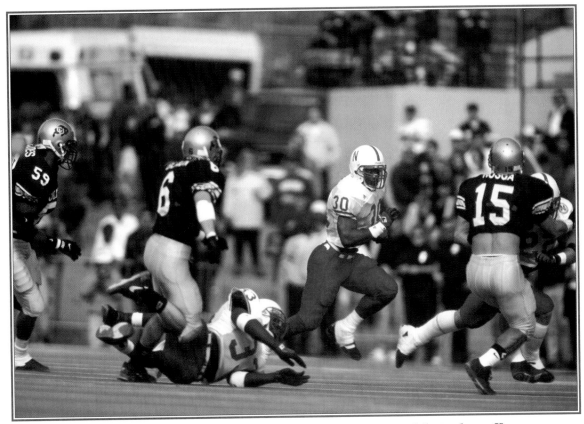

Freshman Ahman Green rushed for 1,086 yards for the powerful Husker offense.

1995 (AP, COACHES)

Osborne's best team, and arguably the best team in college football history, didn't climb to the top of the polls until late October, after back-to-back victories against No. 8 Kansas State (49–25) and No. 7 Colorado (44–21). But there was no question from that point on. The Cornhuskers wrapped up a second consecutive national title and extended their winning streak to a school-record 25 games by hammering coach Steve Spurrier's No. 2–ranked Florida Gators 62–24 in the Fiesta Bowl game.

Nebraska's closest call came against Washington State at home in the fifth game of the season. The Cornhuskers led 28–7 after three quarters, winning 35–21.

The Tommie Frazier–led offense scored 52.4 points per game.

Tommie Frazier, having recovered from the blood clots in 1994, directed an offense that led the nation in rushing (399.8) and scoring (52.4) and ranked second in total yards (556.3). He earned All-America honors and finished a close second to Ohio State's Eddie George in the Heisman Trophy race. Center Aaron Graham and rush end Jared Tomich, who came to Nebraska as a walk-on, also were All-Americans. True freshman I-back Ahman Green rushed for 1,086 yards and 12 touchdowns.

Osborne wasn't able to enjoy his second national championship as much as the first because of some much-publicized, off-the-field problems involving, among others, Phillips.

1997 (COACHES)

The national title was Nebraska's third in four seasons. It provided a fitting conclusion to Osborne's Hall of Fame career. And it depended on some impassioned oratory by senior quarterback Scott Frost, following a 42–17 victory against Tennessee in the Orange Bowl game.

"If you can look at yourself in the mirror and say if your job depended on either playing Michigan or Nebraska, who would you play?" Frost said, addressing his remarks to those who would be voting in the coaches' poll. "It's been split before. It's OK to split it. It should be split."

And in the early-morning hours, the Cornhuskers learned the national title had been

Jason Peter and Grant Wistrom anchored the 1997 Blackshirts.

The 1997 Cornhuskers

split. Michigan was No. 1 in the Associated Press poll. And Nebraska was No. 1 in the coaches' poll.

If not for a dramatic, closer-than-expected 45–38 overtime victory at Missouri in early November, the Cornhuskers probably would have had the title all to themselves. They were ranked No. 1 in both polls going into that game but traded places with Michigan, which went to No. 1 from No. 4 on the strength of a 34–8 victory against No. 2–ranked Penn State.

Nebraska climbed back to No. 2 prior to the Orange Bowl.

Likewise, Michigan might not have had to share the title with a more impressive victory against Washington State in the Rose Bowl game. The Wolverines won 21–16.

Rush end Grant Wistrom, the Lombardi Award winner, defensive tackle Jason Peter and offensive guard Aaron Taylor, the Outland Trophy winner, earned first-team All-America honors.

Lombardi winner Grant Wistrom led a big-play Husker defense.

CONFERENCE CHAMPIONSHIPS (43)

YEAR	CONFERENCE	OVERALL
*1907	1–0–0 (Missouri Valley)	8–2–0
1910	2–0–0 (Missouri Valley)	7–1–0
*1911	2–0–1 (Missouri Valley)	5–1–2
*1912	2–0–0 (Missouri Valley)	7–1–0
*1913	3–0–0 (Missouri Valley)	8–0–0
1914	3–0–0 (Missouri Valley)	7–0–1
1915	4–0–0 (Missouri Valley)	8–0–0
1916	3–1–0 (Missouri Valley)	6–2–0
1917	2–0–0 (Missouri Valley)	5–2–0
1921	3–0–0 (Missouri Valley)	7–1–0
1922	5–0–0 (Missouri Valley)	7–1–0
1923	3–0–2 (Missouri Valley)	4–2–2
1928	5–0–0 (Big Six)	7–1–1
1929	3–0–2 (Big Six)	4–1–3
1931	5–0–0 (Big Six)	8–2–0
1932	5–0–0 (Big Six)	7–1–1
1933	5–0–0 (Big Six)	8–1–0
1935	4–0–1 (Big Six)	6–2–1
1936	5–0–0 (Big Six)	7–2–0
1937	3–0–2 (Big Six)	6–1–2
1940	5–0–0 (Big Six)	8–2–0
1963	7–0–0 (Big Eight)	10–1–0

YEAR	CONFERENCE	OVERALL
1964	6–1–0 (Big Eight)	9–2–0
1965	7–0–0 (Big Eight)	10–1–0
1966	6–1–0 (Big Eight)	9–2–0
*1969	6–1–0 (Big Eight)	9–2–0
1970	7–0–0 (Big Eight)	11–0–1
1971	7–0–0 (Big Eight)	13–0–0
**1972	5–1–1 (Big Eight)	9–2–1
*1975	6–1–0 (Big Eight)	10–2–0
*1978	6–1–0 (Big Eight)	9–3–0
1981	7–0–0 (Big Eight)	9–3–0
1982	7–0–0 (Big Eight)	12–1–0
1983	7–0–0 (Big Eight)	12–1–0
*1984	6–1–0 (Big Eight)	10–2–0
1988	7–0–0 (Big Eight)	11–2–0
*1991	6–0–1 (Big Eight)	9–2–1
1992	6–1–0 (Big Eight)	9–3–0
1993	7–0–0 (Big Eight)	11–1–0
1994	7–0–0 (Big Eight)	13–0–0
1995	7–0–0 (Big Eight)	12–0–0
1997	8–0–0 (Big 12)	13–0–0
1999	7–1–0 (Big 12)	12–1–0

*co-championships

**champion because of three Oklahoma forfeits

Greatest Games

NEBRASKA 20, NOTRE DAME 19
OCTOBER 23, 1915

Knute Rockne, a Notre Dame assistant, had
scouted Guy Chamberlin and thought the
Cornhusker All-American was tipping his hand
when he intended to pass. Rockne was mis-
taken, much to the chagrin of coach Jesse
Harper and the delight of Nebraska fans, who
packed Nebraska Field. Chamberlin scored two
touchdowns, and Loren Caley teamed with
Ted Riddell on a touchdown pass as the
Cornhuskers handed Notre Dame its only loss
of the season, in the first game ever between
the schools. Nebraska coach Ewald O. "Jumbo"
Stiehm, whose teams were a combined
35–2–3 in five seasons, would leave for
Indiana following a third consecutive unbeaten
season.

NEBRASKA 14, NOTRE DAME 6
NOVEMBER 30, 1922

The game was the last at Nebraska Field.
Coming in, the only blemish on Notre Dame's
record was a scoreless tie with Army. Rockne's
team had allowed just 13 points, total, with six
shutouts. Coach Fred Dawson's Cornhuskers
scored both touchdowns in the second quarter,
on a run by Harold "Chick" Hartley and a pass
from Hartley to Dave Noble, who would score
two touchdowns the next year as Nebraska
again defeated Notre Dame, in the third game
played at Memorial Stadium, 14–7. Though
famed sportswriter Grantland Rice wouldn't
give them the nickname until 1924, the legendary "Four Horsemen" played in both
games, the only losses during their collegiate
careers. Their record was 27–2–1.

NEBRASKA 14, MINNESOTA 9
OCTOBER 2, 1937

Defending national champion Minnesota scored on an Andy Uram touchdown pass less than five minutes into Lawrence McCeney "Biff" Jones' first game as Nebraska head coach. That was not a good sign for a capacity crowd at Memorial Stadium. Uram had scored on an 85-yard punt return with 58 seconds remaining to give the Golden Gophers a 7–0 victory at Minneapolis the year before, a typical outcome in a series they dominated. Nebraska was 2–14–2 against them coming in, with its last victory in 1913.

The winning touchdown came on a 25-yard pass from Harris Andrews to Bill Callihan in the fourth quarter. Two plays before, Andrews had passed to Elmer Dohrmann for a 20-yard gain.

NEBRASKA 25, OKLAHOMA 21
OCTOBER 31, 1959

Trick or treat? Cornhusker fans were treated to a dramatic upset for Homecoming. Oklahoma, ranked 19th in the Associated Press poll and more than a two-touchdown favorite, brought a 74-game conference unbeaten streak to Memorial Stadium. Nebraska hadn't beaten the Sooners since 1942 and had been outscored in the previous eight games 313–47. The victory was even sweeter for Cornhusker coach Bill Jennings because he was from Norman, Oklahoma, had played for the Sooners and had been an assistant and coordinated recruiting for Oklahoma coach Bud Wilkinson. Lineman Lee Zentic returned a quick kick for a touchdown to give Nebraska its first lead, and Ron Meade's pass interception in the end zone sealed the victory, setting off a celebration that included Chancellor Clifford Hardin's canceling Monday classes.

NEBRASKA 25, MICHIGAN 13
SEPTEMBER 29, 1962

Cornhusker coach Bob Devaney said in his 1981 autobiography of the victory at Ann Arbor, Michigan: "I'm not sure I don't cherish it as much as any game I ever coached." He and his staff focused on the game in preparing for the season, his first at Nebraska, because of the national prominence of the Big Ten and Michigan's tradition, though they knew the Wolverines were vulnerable because of their inexperience. The availability of Cornhusker fullback and cocaptain Bill "Thunder" Thornton was in doubt because of a dislocated shoulder he suffered during practice three weeks earlier. Thornton played, however, and played well, scoring two touchdowns. The crowd of 70,000-plus was the largest ever to watch Nebraska in a regular-season game at the time.

NEBRASKA 17, LSU 12
JANUARY 1, 1971

Quarterback Jerry Tagge, with a push from center Doug Dumler, stretched the ball across the goal line with 8:50 remaining to give Nebraska the Orange Bowl game victory and, when the Associated Press poll votes were counted, its first national championship. The Cornhuskers started fast, scoring 10 points in the first 13 minutes. But LSU scored its only touchdown on the final play of the third quarter to take a 12–10 lead. The Cornhuskers responded with a Tagge-directed, 13-play, 67-yard touchdown drive, the key play being a 15-yard pass to I-back Jeff Kinney on third-down-and-7 at the LSU 20-yard line. Nebraska's Blackshirt defense locked up the victory, forcing a pair of LSU turnovers in the final minutes. Defensive end Willie Harper recovered a fumble, and then linebacker Bob Terrio intercepted a pass to erase the Tigers' final hope.

NEBRASKA 35, OKLAHOMA 31 NOVEMBER 25, 1971

The Game of the Century on Thanksgiving Day at Norman, Oklahoma, lived up to the hype. Nebraska was ranked No. 1 and led the nation in defense. Oklahoma was ranked No. 2 and led the nation in offense. Both were undefeated and untied. The teams included 17 of the 22 players on the Associated Press All–Big Eight first team, and they had the undivided attention of the nation's college football fans. The finish was appropriately dramatic. Oklahoma took the lead with 7:10 remaining, and the Cornhuskers responded by driving 74 yards on 12 plays, with I-back Jeff Kinney scoring his fourth touchdown on third down from two yards out with 1:38 remaining. The drive's key play was a third-down pass from quarterback Jerry Tagge to wingback Johnny Rodgers. Nebraska middle guard Rich Glover played the game of his life, making 22 tackles. The game of the last century remains a game for the ages.

NEBRASKA 17, OKLAHOMA 14 NOVEMBER 11, 1978

Senior monster back Jim Pillen recovered a Billy Sims fumble at the Nebraska 3-yard line with 3:27 remaining to preserve coach Tom Osborne's first victory against Oklahoma. The Sooners, undefeated, untied and ranked No. 1, fumbled nine times, losing six. Sims, the Heisman Trophy winner that season, lost two of the fumbles in the fourth quarter, as top-ranked Oklahoma tried in vain to overcome a 24-yard Billy Todd field goal with 11:51 remaining. Sims, who had rushed for 200 or more yards in three consecutive games, scored both of the Sooner touchdowns, on runs of 44 and 30 yards. Nebraska countered with touchdown runs by Rick Berns and I.M. Hipp, in the second and third quarters. The victory put the Cornhuskers in position to play Penn State in the Orange Bowl for the national championship. But a week later, Missouri upset Nebraska, also in Lincoln, leading to an Orange Bowl rematch with Oklahoma.

Jeff Kinney's second-quarter TD was one of four he scored during Nebraska's epic 1971 game with Oklahoma.

Turner Gill's failed two-point conversion ended one of the greatest games in college football history.

MIAMI 31, NEBRASKA 30
JANUARY 2, 1984

Osborne almost certainly could have had his first national championship had he been willing to settle for a tie. That was the consensus, anyway. The Cornhuskers, ranked No. 1 throughout the season, would have remained undefeated with a Scott Livingston extra-point kick. But Osborne opted for a 2-point conversion attempt that would have meant victory. Miami's Ken Calhoun deflected Turner Gill's pass enough that it glanced off I-back Jeff Smith incomplete. Nebraska rallied from a 31–17 fourth-quarter deficit, with Smith, who was playing for an injured Mike Rozier, scoring two touchdowns in the final 6:55, the second with 48 seconds remaining. Miami had built a 17–0 first-quarter lead, but the Cornhuskers battled back to tie less than two minutes into the second half. Their first touchdown came when guard Dean Steinkuhler picked up an intentional fumble and ran 19 yards. Nebraska didn't leave the Orange Bowl with a national title, but Osborne and his team left with national respect for playing to win. Said Miami coach Howard Schnellenberger: "This was a championship game, and [Osborne] went after it like a champion."

NEBRASKA 24, MIAMI 17
JANUARY 1, 1995

At halftime of the Orange Bowl game, Osborne reminded the Cornhuskers that if they kept "hammering" away, Miami's defense would wear down. And so it did, though there were some anxious moments among Nebraska fans when the Hurricanes increased their lead to 17–7 less than two minutes into the second half. They wouldn't score again, however. The Cornhuskers got two of the points back quickly, when rush end Dwayne Harris tackled Miami quarterback Frank Costa for a safety.

But the offensive persistence didn't begin to pay off until midway through the fourth quarter, when fullback Cory Schlesinger scored two touchdowns in a span of 4 minutes and 52 seconds to give Osborne his first national championship. Tommie Frazier, who had been sidelined by blood clots throughout Big Eight play, returned to start at quarterback. But Brook Berringer got Nebraska on the scoreboard with a 19-yard pass to tight end Mark Gilman in the second quarter, after Miami had jumped out to a 10–0 lead on their home field.

Jason Jenkins carries teammate Tom Seiler off the field after Nebraska's breakthrough Orange Bowl win over Miami.

NEBRASKA 45, MISSOURI 38 (OT)
NOVEMBER 8, 1997

Everyone remembers the final play in regulation, Matt Davison's touchdown catch of a ball thrown by Scott Frost that deflected off the foot of Shevin Wiggins. But what preceded the catch at Missouri's Faurot Field was dramatic as well. With 1:02 remaining, Nebraska took over at its own 33-yard line. Nine plays later, without benefit of timeouts, Frost had directed the Cornhuskers to the Missouri 12-yard line. Only seven seconds remained. The tying touchdown came on third down.

Nebraska lost the coin toss and had the ball first in overtime, scoring in three plays, the third a 12-yard run by Frost for his fourth touchdown. He finished with a career-high 141 rushing yards, and I-back Ahman Green rushed for 189 as the Cornhuskers rolled up 528 total yards. Missouri gained 386 yards, with quarterback Corby Jones accounting for 293 passing and rushing. The Tigers went ahead 38–31 with 4:39 remaining.

NEBRASKA 27,
NOTRE DAME 24 (OT)
SEPTEMBER 9, 2000

Quarterback Eric Crouch, who would win the Heisman Trophy a year later, ran seven yards for a touchdown in overtime to give the No. 1–ranked Cornhuskers the overtime victory at South Bend, Indiana. The touchdown was his third. But the game's biggest play,

according to Crouch, was his nine-yard pass to tight end Tracey Wistrom on a third-and-9 from the Notre Dame 24-yard line to keep Nebraska alive in overtime. Defensive tackle Jeremy Slechta also made a big play in overtime, sacking Fighting Irish quarterback Arnaz Battle on third-and-goal at the Cornhusker 4-yard line to force a field goal.

Bobby Newcombe and the Huskers woke up some echoes of their own with an OT win in South Bend.

One of college football's signature plays: Johnny Rodgers' 72-yard punt return for a TD vs. Oklahoma in 1971.

Greatest Moments

REYNOLDS' RUN
NOVEMBER 4, 1950

Bobby Reynolds scored 22 touchdowns during his sophomore season. But none was more spectacular than the third of three in a 40–34 Cornhusker victory against Missouri, to the delight of a Homecoming crowd of 38,000 at Memorial Stadium. On fourth-and-3 at the Missouri 33-yard line, Reynolds took a direct snap from center in a single-wing formation and dropped back as if to pass. He was under heavy pressure, however, and began running. He gave ground across the 50-yard line and into his own territory, near the 45, reversing field twice and then running down the west sideline for the touchdown.

RODGERS' RETURN
NOVEMBER 25, 1971

Less than four minutes into the Game of the Century, Johnny Rodgers turned a punt from Oklahoma's Joe Wylie into what was arguably the signature play in Cornhusker history. The 72-yard touchdown return opened the scoring in Nebraska's 35–31 victory at Owen Field. A crowd of 61,826 as well as millions watching on ABC television witnessed the play, one of eight punt-return touchdowns during Rodgers' three seasons (counting one in the 1972 Orange Bowl game against Alabama). Cornhusker cornerback Joe Blahak made the final block on the play. Sooner fans still maintain Blahak's block on Jon Harrison was a clip. Blahak responds with a question: "Did the official throw a flag? Then there was no clip."

"MICHAEL HEISMAN"
SEPTEMBER 24, 1983

Mike Rozier was credited with a two-yard touchdown run in the third quarter of a 42–10 victory against UCLA, before a Memorial Stadium crowd of 76,510. But he ran an estimated 75 to 80 yards before finally crossing the goal line. The play was a "49 pitch" on second-down-and-goal at the Bruins' 2-yard line. Rozier took the pitch from quarterback Turner Gill and ran to his left, giving ground to the 6, where he reversed field. He dropped back to the 18-yard line before angling toward the end zone, breaking tackles and utilizing blocks, including one from Gill, as he went. Afterward, teammate Irving Fryar, a wingback, told reporters: "He can do anything he wants. He's 'Michael Heisman.'" The play, shown to a national television audience on ESPN, enhanced his candidacy for the Heisman Trophy, which he won.

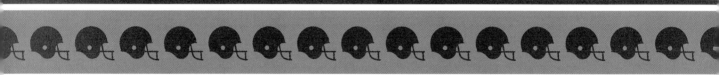

FRAZIER FRUSTRATES FLORIDA
JANUARY 2, 1996

The play didn't appear all that special at first. On second-and-5 from his own 25-yard line late in the third quarter of the Fiesta Bowl game against No. 2–ranked Florida, quarterback Tommie Frazier faked a handoff to fullback Brian Schuster and for a split-second appeared to consider a pitch to I-back Clinton Childs. He kept the ball, however, and ran 75 yards for the touchdown that defined his Cornhusker career. He broke seven or eight tackles during the first 20 yards, after which he was untouched by a Gator defender. "They kept contacting me, but I kept my legs going," Frazier explained following the 62–24 victory that gave Nebraska a second consecutive national championship.

Greatest team ever?
A 62–24 win over
Florida offered
convincing evidence.

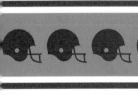

*Tommie Frazier dazzled
the Fiesta Bowl crowd
with this third-quarter
TD sprint.*

Scott Frost celebrates the unlikeliest of wins: Nebraska's 45–38 "Missouri Miracle."

MISSOURI MIRACLE
NOVEMBER 8, 1997

Matt Davison, who was playing in only the eighth game of his Cornhusker career, was in the right place at the right time on the final play in regulation at Missouri's Faurot Field. Top-ranked Nebraska trailed 38–31 with seven seconds on the clock and the ball at the Missouri 12-yard line. The play was a "99 double slant" pass, with Davison and Lance Brown slanting from one side and Shevin Wiggins and Kenny Cheatham slanting from the other. Quarterback Scott Frost looked in the direction of Davison and Brown then turned and sent the pass toward Wiggins. The ball popped up; Wiggins deflected it, kicking it as a soccer player might and sending it to the back of the end zone, where Davison lunged, caught the ball as he landed on his stomach, then jumped up to display the ball. Kris Brown added the extra-point kick. The Cornhuskers won in overtime, 45–38, on the way to a national championship.

Eric Crouch enhanced his Heisman candidacy with one of the most memorable plays in Husker history.

BLACK 41 FLASH REVERSE PASS
OCTOBER 27, 2001

Midway through the fourth quarter at Memorial Stadium, with a 13–10 lead against Oklahoma on first-and-10 at his own 37-yard line, Nebraska quarterback Eric Crouch handed to wingback Thunder Collins, who had gone in motion to his right. Collins pitched the ball to Mike Stuntz, who was running the opposite direction. Stuntz, a true freshman recruited as a quarterback, pulled up and passed to Crouch, who had slipped behind the secondary. He caught the ball near the Sooners' 39-yard line and raced to the end zone. The play capped the 20–10 upset of No. 2–ranked Oklahoma and added a highlight to Crouch's Heisman Trophy résumé. Oklahoma had tried a similar play late in the first half, but it hadn't worked.

NEVER GIVE UP
DECEMBER 28, 2005

The play wasn't over. And fortunately for Nebraska, Titus Brothers and Zack Bowman wanted to make sure Michigan tight end Tyler Ecker didn't get to the end zone. The Alamo Bowl game's final play began at the Michigan 36-yard line, with two seconds remaining and Nebraska leading 32–28. Wolverine quarterback Chad Henne passed to wide receiver Jason Avant, who initiated a game of keep-away with the first of several laterals and pitches back and forth. When center Mark Bihl couldn't catch a toss across the field, Nebraska players began running on the field in celebration, accompanied by reporters and photographers. Coach Bill Callahan received the obligatory drenching. The ball was still live, however. Michigan's Mike Hart picked it up and pitched to Ecker, who ran goal-ward along the Michigan sideline as Wolverine players and coaches came onto the field as well. Brothers and Bowman finally caught Ecker at the Nebraska 13-yard line, knocking him down and out of bounds to preserve a victory that signaled Nebraska's return to college football prominence.

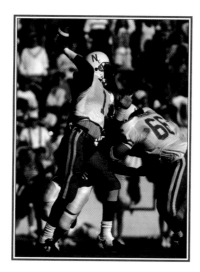

THE RIVALRIES

For many teams, the Nebraska game is marked in red on the schedule every year. Some great rivalries have helped define Nebraska football and have given fans many of their greatest memories.

An estimated 20,000 to 25,000 Nebraska fans were among a crowd of 80,232 at Notre Dame Stadium to watch the Cornhuskers pull out a 27–24 overtime victory and spoil Notre Dame's upset bid in 2000. Even though Nebraska's allotment was only 4,000 tickets, Cornhusker fans found a way in, reflecting their willingness to travel in support of the team and echoing a brief rivalry long past.

Nebraska first played Notre Dame in 1915, "Jumbo" Stiehm's final season as coach. The Cornhuskers won at Lincoln, 20–19.

Teams from the schools played each of the next 10 seasons, with only two of the games in South Bend. After the 1925 game in Lincoln, however, Notre Dame suddenly terminated the series, citing anti-Irish-Catholic sentiment and poor treatment of its fans and school officials.

At that point, the series was even, at 5–5–1. Notre Dame's famed Four Horsemen lost only twice during their college careers, both against Nebraska—in 1922 (14–6) and again in 1923 (14–7).

The Huskers have dominated their rivals to the south in the longest continuous series in Division I-A.

The schools have met on a football field only five times since 1925, with the Cornhuskers winning the last three, including a 40-6 victory in the 1973 Orange Bowl, Bob Devaney's final game as coach.

Nebraska's early rivals also included Iowa, Minnesota and Pittsburgh.

The Iowa rivalry, one of proximity, began in 1891, Nebraska's second season. The first 10 games were played at Omaha, including two in three days in 1896. Iowa appeared on Nebraska's schedule regularly but not annually—and not at all during the 1920s—through 1946. The Cornhuskers and Hawkeyes have played only six times since 1946. Nebraska leads the series 26–12–3.

In the early 1900s, Minnesota and Pittsburgh were national powers against which Nebraska measured itself, and not always to the satisfaction of its fans. Victories against

either of the two were rare and cause for celebration. Both still hold advantages in their
series with the Cornhuskers.

From the beginning of the series in 1900
through 1954, Minnesota had a commanding
lead, 28–5–2. Nebraska has narrowed the gap,
winning the last 14, including an 84–13 victory
at Minneapolis in 1983. But the schools have

met only four times since 1974. Pittsburgh
leads its series with Nebraska 15–6–3. The
schools have played only twice since 1958,
with the Cornhuskers winning both.

None of those budding rivalries blossomed.
The earliest series that have survived are those
against Kansas and Missouri, which joined
Nebraska and Iowa in forming the Western

Nebraska has controlled its latter-day rivalry with Colorado.

Inter-State University Football Association in 1892. The short-lived association lasted only through 1897.

Nebraska played Kansas for the first time in 1892 in a series that ranks as the third-longest in NCAA Division I-A history—112 games through 2005. Only Minnesota-Wisconsin and Kansas-Missouri are longer. Nebraska-Kansas is the longest continuous series in Division I-A, with games every season since 1906. The rivalry aspect of the series has been diminished by Nebraska's dominance, however. It didn't lose to the Jayhawks from 1917 to 1943, with only three ties during that period, and it put together a 36-game winning streak in the series that the Jayhawks finally were able to break at Lawrence in 2005.

Nebraska also was scheduled to play Missouri for the first time in 1892, but Missouri forfeited rather than compete against George Flippin, one of the first African-American football players at a predominantly white college or university. Nebraska's series with Missouri has been continuous since 1922.

Nebraska dominated the series early, losing only six of the first 31 games through

1937. Missouri dominated in the 1940s and 1950s, and the Tigers continued to hold their own in the 1960s and 1970s, handing Bob Devaney and Tom Osborne their first losses as Cornhusker head coaches.

The fact that Devaney and Missouri coach Dan Devine (1957–1970) were assistants at Michigan State under Duffy Daugherty added a personal element to the rivalry, as did the fact that Warren Powers, an assistant at Nebraska under both Devaney and Osborne as well as a player on Devaney's first team, became the Tigers' coach in the late 1970s. His first Missouri team cost Nebraska a shot at playing for the national championship, in fact, upsetting the No. 2–ranked Cornhuskers in the final game of the 1978 regular season, 35–31. Nebraska wouldn't lose to the Tigers again until 2003, giving it a decided series advantage.

Though the Cornhuskers have never really bought into it, former Colorado coach Bill McCartney designated them Colorado's rival soon after he took the job. The designation, which fostered hatred, put Nebraska in red letters on the schedule and even led to a prohibition against red vehicles in the athletic

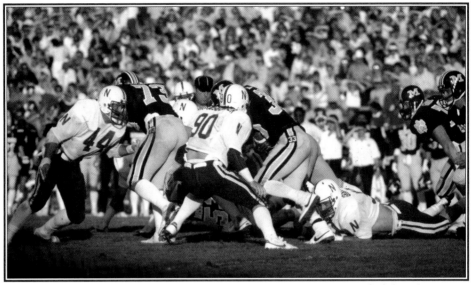

After Missouri cost Nebraska a shot at the 1978 national title, the Huskers won 24 straight in the series.

department, was surprising given that Nebraska had won 14 consecutive games in the series.

In the five games before McCartney arrived in Boulder, the Cornhuskers had outscored Colorado 227–46, and over the course of the 14 victories, the average score was 36–11. Nebraska's winning streak would continue through McCartney's first four seasons, including a 69–19 victory in 1983.

The Buffalos finally broke through in 1986, with a 20–10 upset, and they won in 1989 and 1990 (on the way to a national championship).

But after a tie in 1991, Nebraska again took control.

Colorado shattered the No. 2–ranked Cornhuskers' national championship dreams in 2001, handing them their first loss in the final game of the regular season, by a stunning 62–36 margin. The Buffalos' Big 12 championship rings included an inscription of the score. But Nebraska exacted revenge in 2005, shocking the Buffaloes at home 30–3 and effectively ending Gary Barnett's tenure as coach.

—— Big Red South ——

Ask any longtime Cornhusker fan about a rival and there will be one answer—Oklahoma. But the structure of the Big 12 Conference has diminished the rivalry, reducing what was the Big Eight's annual showcase on Thanksgiving weekend to two inter-divisional games every four years.

Oklahoma's main rival has always been Texas, of course. But the Sooners were Nebraska's chief rival, dating to at least 1959 and a 25–21 Cornhusker victory.

Coach Bud Wilkinson's Oklahoma team came to Lincoln with a 74-game conference unbeaten streak on Halloween in 1959 to play Nebraska, which was coached by Bill Jennings, who had played at Oklahoma and then had been an assistant under Wilkinson. Although Notre Dame had snapped the Sooners' NCAA-record 47-game winning streak in 1957, Oklahoma continued to dominate the Big Seven.

The Cornhuskers were unlikely streak-breakers, having lost 16 in a row to Oklahoma, beginning in 1943. They were 2–4 going into the game, after winning only four of 20 games in Jennings' first two seasons as head coach. And they had managed only three winning seasons since 1940.

The victory set off a wild celebration that included the razing of Memorial Stadium's goal posts and university classes being cancelled the following Monday. It also provided a foundation for a rivalry that would help define the Big Eight, which was established a year later.

The Nebraska-Oklahoma series began in 1912, and the teams played each other every season from 1928 through 1997. The Cornhuskers dominated early, winning 16 of the first 22 games and shutting out Oklahoma 11 times. The Sooners won only three times during that stretch.

Ironically, the second game between the schools in 1919 briefly cost Nebraska its conference affiliation. The Missouri Valley Conference, of which Nebraska was an original member, prohibited the scheduling of games in

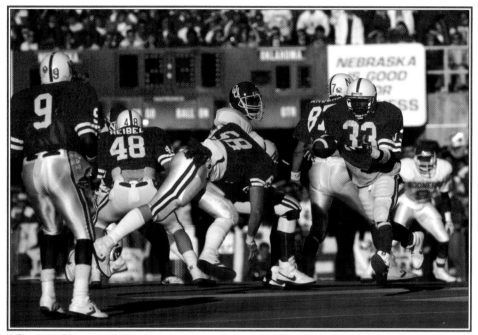

The Huskers and Sooners won or shared 32 of 36 Big Eight titles.

places other than where schools were located. But Nebraska scheduled a game against the Sooners at Omaha, as part of a double-header that included Creighton-Marquette.

As a result, the Cornhuskers were forced to withdraw from the conference and played as independents in 1919 and 1920, when Kansas was the only conference school willing to schedule Nebraska. The conference, which had added Oklahoma in 1920, readmitted Nebraska in 1921.

The Sooners played in the first game at Nebraska's Memorial Stadium in 1923, losing 24–0. Nebraska would dedicate the stadium a week later against Kansas, with a scoreless tie.

Nebraska and Oklahoma began playing on an annual basis with the formation of the Big Six in 1928. The Big Six lasted 20 years, with Nebraska winning nine championships. Oklahoma, which won three Big Six titles and shared two others, dominated the successor to the Big Six, winning all 12 Big Seven titles. The

Nebraska game in 1959 was the only Big Seven game the Sooners lost.

The rivalry was a result of the two programs' success as much as anything. In the Big Eight's 36 seasons, Nebraska and Oklahoma won or shared 32 of the championships. And their annual showdown typically had national championship as well as conference title implications.

They won a combined four national championships during the 1970s, and they might have had a fifth if the Cornhuskers hadn't upset the top-ranked Sooners 17–14 at Lincoln in 1978. Oklahoma's Barry Switzer called the 1978 team possibly the best during his tenure as coach, which included three national championships. The Sooners avenged the loss in the Orange Bowl, winning an unexpected rematch 31–24.

Osborne and Switzer were assistants at the schools for the Game of the Century at Norman in 1971, the rivalry's most memorable game, at least from Nebraska's point of view. The Cornhuskers won the matchup between the nation's No. 1– and No. 2–ranked teams in dramatic fashion, 35–31. The Sooners won what was billed as the Game of the Century II at Lincoln in 1987, handily, 17–7.

Tommie Frazier's Huskers never lost to OU.

"He wouldn't let on that it meant more, but it went unsaid, I guess. It was always more tense. There was more anxiety on the coaching staff before the Oklahoma game." —ALL-AMERICA CENTER MARK TRAYNOWICZ (1982–1984) ON COACH TOM OSBORNE AND OKLAHOMA

Oklahoma was a source of frustration for Osborne. He and Switzer both became head coaches in 1973, and he endured six losses before the upset in 1978. Afterward, Cornhusker fans swarmed the field and pulled down the goal posts. The last time that had happened was in 1959, said Devaney, Nebraska's athletic director, so "we ought to be able to afford new goal posts once every 20 years."

Two years earlier, the Sooners had snatched victory from Nebraska, which appeared to be Orange Bowl–bound, with an unlikely finish that included a lateral and pass for 47 yards followed by a pass and lateral that took the ball to the Cornhusker 2-yard line, from where, with 38 seconds remaining, Oklahoma's Elvis Peacock scored the winning touchdown. Final score, 20–17.

In 1986, Oklahoma won by the same score, and in similar fashion, rallying from a 17–10 deficit in the final minutes. Tim Lashar kicked a 31-yard field goal to win it with six seconds left. "I don't think it was a comeback," Sooner linebacker Brian Bosworth told reporters afterward. "It was just a matter of destiny." Switzer called it "Sooner Magic," a term that would have applied to the 1976 rally as well.

The magic, which had more to do with talent, suddenly ran out with Switzer's departure. Osborne's record against Switzer was 5–11. From 1988 to 1997, however, the Cornhuskers won nine times to even out his career record against Oklahoma at 13–13. Nebraska won Osborne's final two games against the Sooners in 1996 and 1997 by a combined 142–28. The 1997 victory was No. 250 of his career.

Osborne's success against Oklahoma, as well as his success overall, was the result in part of his decision to play the way the Sooners did offensively, with athletic quarterbacks and an option-based attack. He began moving in that direction with his offense in the late 1970s, attracting quarterbacks such as Turner Gill, Steve Taylor, Tommie Frazier and Scott Frost, who transferred from Stanford.

Oklahoma knocked coach Frank Solich's third Nebraska team from No. 1 in the AP rankings in 2000, and the Cornhuskers returned the favor a year later, upsetting No. 2 Oklahoma 20–10. But the rivalry, which was built on mutual respect rather than hatred, isn't as spirited in the Big 12, with the teams not facing off in two out of every four seasons.

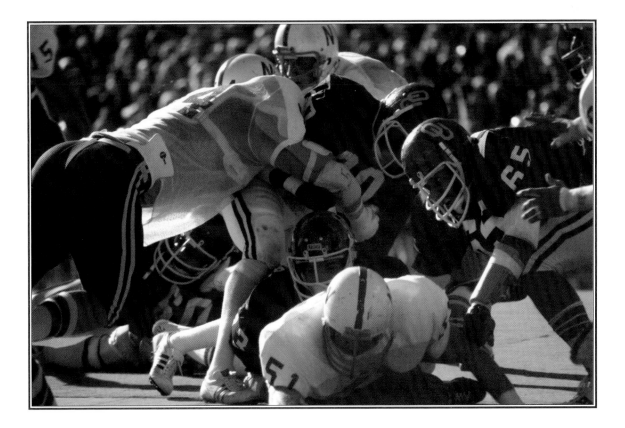

TALKIN' HUSKER FOOTBALL

Here are a few well-chosen words, most from those who have been directly involved in the Cornhusker experience.

"The Nebraska Cornhuskers lost the game, but not their dignity. *For that they can thank their coach, Tom Osborne. No other coach I can immediately think of embodied good coaching principles more or served as a better model of correctitude to his players."* —UNITED PRESS INTERNATIONAL'S MILTON RICHMAN FOLLOWING THE 1984 ORANGE BOWL GAME IN WHICH OSBORNE OPTED FOR A FAILED TWO-POINT CONVERSION ATTEMPT INSTEAD OF SETTLING FOR AN ALMOST-CERTAIN TIE WITH MIAMI

"There have been more nice things said about me in the last month than there were the preceding 25 years." —TOM OSBORNE BEFORE HIS RETIREMENT BECAME OFFICIAL ON FEBRUARY 4, 1998

"Trophies and whistles and bells and rings *don't excite me that much. What really excites me is playing as well as you can, getting the most out of your football team, doing it a certain way."* —COACH TOM OSBORNE PRIOR TO WINNING HIS FIRST NATIONAL CHAMPIONSHIP IN 1994

"He put his heart into his work for all those years, *and there isn't one of us who played for him who doesn't owe him their heart in return."* —FORMER CORNHUSKER AND NFL DEFENSIVE LINEMAN NEIL SMITH ON THE NIGHT IN THE SPRING OF 1998 WHEN TOM OSBORNE FIELD WAS DEDICATED

"When I scored, I looked at the grass in the end zone *and it was a lot greener than anywhere else on the field."* —FULLBACK CORY SCHLESINGER (1992–1994) ON SCORING THE WINNING TOUCHDOWN AGAINST MIAMI IN THE 1995 ORANGE BOWL GAME TO GIVE COACH TOM OSBORNE HIS FIRST NATIONAL CHAMPIONSHIP

"Coach [Tom] Osborne made me a student of the game. That's why it was easy for me to make that transition to be a professional athlete." —FORMER CORNHUSKER AND NFL RUNNING BACK ROGER CRAIG (1980–1982)

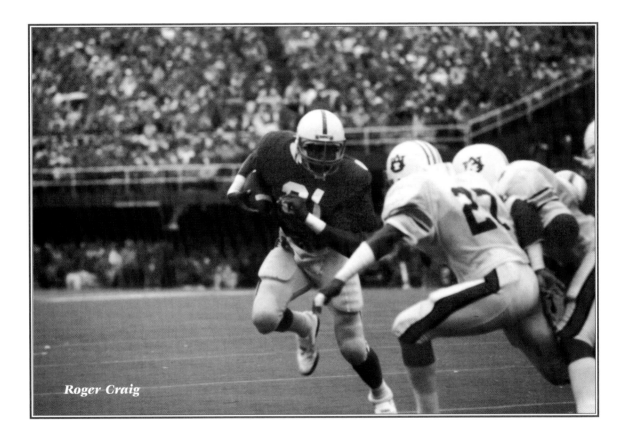

Roger Craig

"Tom's a very nice, very gentle man. But he's very demanding of our players. Everybody's got to do it. There are no shortcuts: pursuit on defense, everybody blocks on offense. I can't remember a game where he didn't talk about that." —FORMER CORNHUSKER RECEIVERS COACH RON BROWN ON TOM OSBORNE

"He thought all of us live on farms, *that we're all big plowboys."*
—Two-time Outland Trophy and Lombardi Award–winning center Dave Rimington (1979–1982) on meeting Dan Marino at an All-American get-together

"No matter where I go, where I end up, this place is always going to be home to me. If I could do it all over again, I wouldn't be wearing any other colors but the red and white."

—TWO-TIME ALL-AMERICAN AND ACADEMIC ALL-AMERICAN RUSH END GRANT WISTROM (1994–1997)

"Duffy [Daugherty] thought this was a better job than I did; I was very reluctant about it, in fact, but he seemed certain this could be a good deal. He told me if I won here as I had been able to win at Wyoming, things could go big." —COACH BOB DEVANEY IN HIS 1981 AUTOBIOGRAPHY

"We never felt like we were going to lose a game. Coach [Bob] Devaney may have scared us a few times into thinking we might, just to be ready and prepared. But we always felt confident that once we got out there, we were ready to go." —FRED DUDA (1963–1965), FORMER CORNHUSKER QUARTERBACK

"Seeing that ball, my eyes got bigger and bigger. All I could think of was catching the ball. I fell straight down, didn't run. All I wanted to do was catch it and hold onto it." —ALL–BIG EIGHT LINEBACKER BOB TERRIO (1970–1971) ON INTERCEPTING A PASS WITH 45 SECONDS REMAINING TO SEAL THE 1972 ORANGE BOWL VICTORY AGAINST LSU THAT GAVE COACH BOB DEVANEY AND NEBRASKA THEIR FIRST NATIONAL CHAMPIONSHIP

"I never thought about being the top running back at Nebraska. I just wanted to be remembered as a good running back who came through Nebraska." —I-BACK AHMAN GREEN (1995–1997), THE SECOND-LEADING RUSHER IN CORNHUSKER HISTORY WITH 3,880 YARDS IN THREE SEASONS

"We were raised in a different time. *We didn't dance in the end zone. The most daring thing we did was wear white shoes. Dick Davis, Mike Green and I got white shoes. I dyed mine black right away."* —I-BACK JOE ORDUNA (1967–1970), THE LEADING RUSHER ON NEBRASKA'S FIRST NATIONAL CHAMPIONSHIP TEAM

"The greatest moment in my life *was winning a scholarship to come to Nebraska. I just want to tell you fans how much I love you all."* —OUTLAND TROPHY AND LOMBARDI AWARD WINNER RICH GLOVER (1970–1972), SPEAKING, TEARFULLY, AT A CORNHUSKER BANQUET IN 1982

"I've never been more excited at practice, ever. *I've been going to these games since I was about two or three years old. I know the players who have had these."* —MIDDLE LINEBACKER BARRETT RUUD (2001–2004), THE CORNHUSKERS' CAREER TACKLES LEADER, ON WEARING A BLACKSHIRT FOR THE FIRST TIME

"If you held a block for a second, [Mike] *Rozier was through the hole."*
—ALL-AMERICA CENTER MARK TRAYNOWICZ (1982–1984) ON HEISMAN TROPHY WINNER MIKE
ROZIER, THE CORNHUSKERS' CAREER RUSHING LEADER

"Even I'd get excited when John would stand back there, ready to field a punt. In my mind, Rodgers was the greatest punt-return man I've ever seen in college football. Every time he touched the ball, he was a threat to go all the way." —BOB DEVANEY IN HIS 1981 AUTOBIOGRAPHY, DESCRIBING THE EXCITEMENT GENERATED BY HEISMAN TROPHY WINNER JOHNNY RODGERS

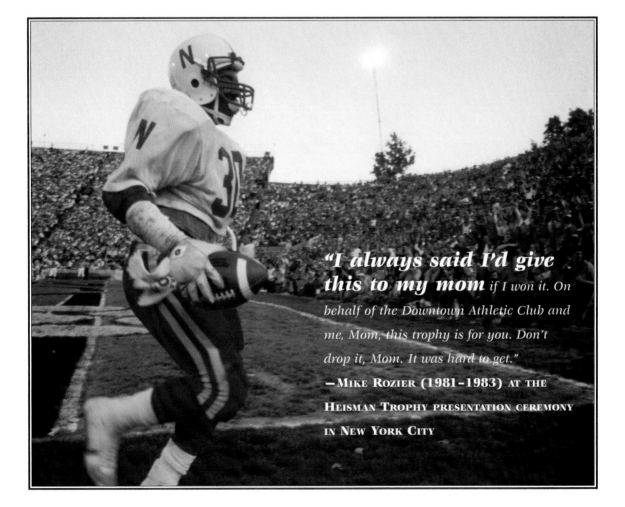

"I always said I'd give this to my mom if I won it. On behalf of the Downtown Athletic Club and me, Mom, this trophy is for you. Don't drop it, Mom. It was hard to get." —MIKE ROZIER (1981–1983) AT THE HEISMAN TROPHY PRESENTATION CEREMONY IN NEW YORK CITY

"[Monte] Kiffin didn't miss anything. *And the first thing you learned your first year was, keep your mouth shut. You never say anything, ever. I don't care if you were a senior or what. Monte was going to say something, and you never said a word."* —DEFENSIVE END STEVE MANSTEDT (1971–1973) ON FORMER CORNHUSKER DEFENSIVE LINE COACH AND LATER DEFENSIVE COORDINATOR MONTE KIFFIN

"I was such a fighter *that it didn't bother me if people didn't want me here. I wanted to play football for Nebraska, so whatever I had to take to do that is what I did."* —CHARLES BRYANT (1953–1954), ONE OF THE FIRST AFRICAN-AMERICANS TO EARN A FOOTBALL LETTER AT NEBRASKA IN THE MODERN ERA

"When I was at Nebraska, there was great enthusiasm... *people thought we ought to be going to a bowl game, that we ought to be doing this and that."* —FORREST BEHM (1938–1940), AN ALL-AMERICA LINEMAN ON THE CORNHUSKERS' 1941 ROSE BOWL TEAM

FACTS AND FIGURES

Nebraska Bowl Game Scores

RECORD: 22-21			
DATE	BOWL	OPPONENT	RESULT
January 1, 1941	Rose	Stanford	L 21–13
January 1, 1955	Orange	Duke	L 34–7
December 15, 1962	Gotham	Miami	W 36–34
January 1, 1964	Orange	Auburn	W 13–7
January 1, 1965	Cotton	Arkansas	L 10–7
January 1, 1966	Orange	Alabama	L 39–28
January 2, 1967	Sugar	Alabama	L 34–7
December 20, 1969	Sun	Georgia	W 45–6
January 1, 1971*	Orange	Louisiana State	W 17–12
January 1, 1972*	Orange	Alabama	W 38–6
January 1, 1973	Orange	Notre Dame	W 40–6
January 1, 1974	Cotton	Texas	W 19–3
December 31, 1974	Sugar	Florida	W 13–10
December 26, 1975	Fiesta	Arizona State	L 17–14
December 31, 1976	Astro-Bluebonnet	Texas Tech	W 27–24
December 19, 1977	Liberty	North Carolina	W 21–17

DATE	BOWL	OPPONENT	RESULT
January 1, 1979	Orange	Oklahoma	L 31–24
January 1, 1980	Cotton	Houston	L 17–14
December 27, 1980	Sun	Mississippi State	W 31–17
January 1, 1982	Orange	Clemson	L 22–15
January 1, 1983	Orange	Louisiana State	W 21–20
January 2, 1984	Orange	Miami	L 31–30
January 1, 1985	Sugar	Louisiana State	W 28–10
January 1, 1986	Fiesta	Michigan	L 27–23
January 1, 1987	Sugar	Louisiana State	W 30–15
January 1, 1988	Fiesta	Florida State	L 31–28
January 2, 1989	Orange	Miami	L 23–3
January 1, 1990	Fiesta	Florida State	L 41–17
January 1, 1991	Citrus	Georgia Tech	L 45–21
January 1, 1992	Orange	Miami	L 22–0
January 1, 1993	Orange	Florida State	L 27–14
January 1, 1994	Orange	Florida State	L 18–16
January 1, 1995*	Orange	Miami	W 24–17
January 2, 1996*	Fiesta	Florida	W 62–24
December 31, 1996	Orange	Virginia Tech	W 41–21
January 2, 1998*	Orange	Tennessee	W 42–17
December 30, 1998	Holiday	Arizona	L 23–20
January 2, 2000	Fiesta	Tennessee	W 31–21
December 30, 2000	Alamo	Northwestern	W 66–17
January 3, 2002	Rose	Miami	L 37–14
December 27, 2002	Independence	Mississippi	L 27–23
December 29, 2003	Alamo	Michigan State	W 17–3
December 28, 2005	Alamo	Michigan	W 32–28

* National Champions

Career Statistical Leaders

Rushes: 668, Mike Rozier, 1981–1983

Rushing Yards: 4,780, Mike Rozier, 1981–1983

Rushing Yards per Game: 136.6, Mike Rozier, 1981–1983

Rushing Touchdowns: 59, Eric Crouch, 1998–2001

Pass Attempts: 637, Dave Humm, 1972–1974

Pass Completions: 353, Dave Humm, 1972–1974

Passing Yards: 5,035, Dave Humm, 1972–1974

Passing Touchdowns: 43, Tommie Frazier, 1992–1995

Receptions: 143, Johnny Rodgers, 1970–1972

Receiving Yards: 2,479, Johnny Rodgers, 1970–1972

Touchdown Receptions: 25, Johnny Rodgers, 1970–1972

Total Offense Yards: 7,915, Eric Crouch, 1998–2001

Points Scored: 388, Kris Brown, 1995–1998

Punt-Return Average (Min. 25): 18.33 yards, Pat Fischer, 1958–1960

Kickoff-Return Average (Min. 12): 28.29 yards, Tyrone Hughes, 1989–1992

Total Tackles: 432, Barrett Ruud, 2001–2004

Sacks: 29.5, Trev Alberts, 1990–1993

Interceptions: 14, Dana Stephenson, 1967–1969

——— Huskers in the Pros ———

Titus Adams	DT	New York Jets
Ryon Bingham	DT	San Diego Chargers
Josh Brown	K	Seattle Seahawks
Kris Brown	K	Houston Texans
Mike Brown	SS	Chicago Bears
Ralph Brown	CB	Minnesota Vikings
Correll Buckhalter	RB	Philadelphia Eagles
Daniel Bullocks	S	Detroit Lions
Josh Bullocks	S	New Orleans Saints
Seppo Evwaraye	OT	Carolina Panthers
Toniu Fonoti	OG	Minnesota Vikings
Aaron Golliday	TE	Kansas City Chiefs
Ahman Green	RB	Green Bay Packers
DeJuan Groce	CB	St. Louis Rams
Russ Hochstein	OG	New England Patriots
Richie Incognito	C	St. Louis Rams
Trevor Johnson	DE	New York Jets
Chris Kelsay	DE	Buffalo Bills
Sam Koch	P	Baltimore Ravens
Jammal Lord	S	Houston Texans
Mike Minter	S	Carolina Panthers
Jerrell Pippens	S	San Diego Chargers
Carlos Polk	LB	San Diego Chargers
Dominic Raiola	C	Detroit Lions
Cory Ross	RB	Baltimore Ravens
Mike Rucker	DE	Carolina Panthers

Barrett Ruud	LB	Tampa Bay Buccaneers
Cory Schlesinger	FB	Detroit Lions
Scott Shanle	LB	Dallas Cowboys
Will Shields	OG	Kansas City Chiefs
Le Kevin Smith	DT	New England Patriots
Benard Thomas	DE	Baltimore Ravens
Adam Treu	C	Oakland Raiders
Kyle Vanden Bosch	DE	Tennessee Titans
Eric Warfield	CB	Kansas City Chiefs
Fabian Washington	CB	Oakland Raiders
Zach Wiegert	OT	Houston Texans
Demorrio Williams	LB	Atlanta Falcons
Grant Wistrom	DE	Seattle Seahawks

Mike Brown

First-Round Draft Picks

2004	CB	Fabian Washington, Oakland Raiders
1998	RE	Grant Wistrom, St. Louis Rams
	DT	Jason Peter, Carolina Panthers
1997	CB	Michael Booker, Atlanta Falcons
1996	RB	Lawrence Phillips, St. Louis Rams
1994	OLB	Trev Alberts, Indianapolis Colts
1992	TE	Johnny Mitchell, New York Jets
1991	DB	Bruce Pickens, Atlanta Falcons
	OLB	Mike Croel, Denver Broncos
1989	OLB	Broderick Thomas, Tampa Bay Buccaneers
1988	DE	Neil Smith, Kansas City Chiefs
1987	MG	Danny Noonan, Dallas Cowboys
1984	WR	Irving Fryar, New England Patriots
	OG	Dean Steinkuhler, Houston Oilers
	RB	Mike Rozier, Houston Oilers *
1983	C	Dave Rimington, Cincinnati Bengals
1982	LB	Jimmy Williams, Detroit Lions
1980	TE	Junior Miller, Atlanta Falcons
1979	DE	George Andrews, Los Angeles Rams
	OT	Kelvin Clark, Denver Broncos
1975	LB	Tom Ruud, Buffalo Bills
1974	DT	John Dutton, Baltimore Colts

1973	HB	Johnny Rodgers, San Diego Chargers
1972	HB	Jeff Kinney, Kansas City Chiefs
	QB	Jerry Tagge, Green Bay Packers
	DT	Larry Jacobson, New York Giants
1964	G	Bob Brown, Philadelphia Eagles
	T	Lloyd Voss, Green Bay Packers
1937	FB	Sam Francis, Philadelphia Eagles
	HB	Lloyd Cardwell, Detroit Lions
	E	Les McDonald, Chicago Bears

*supplemental draft

Academic All-Americans

Nebraska leads the nation in Academic All-Americans, with 50 players earning first-team recognition, 12 of them earning it twice.

Ted Harvey	DB	1976–1977
Randy Schleusener	OG	1979–1980
Dave Rimington	C	1981–1982
Scott Strasburger	DE	1983–1984
Rob Stuckey	DT	1983–1984
Mark Blazek	S	1987–1988
Mike Stigge	P	1991–1992
Terry Connealy	NT	1993–1994
Rob Zatechka	OT	1993–1994
Grant Wistrom	RE	1996–1997
Joel Makovicka	FB	1997–1998
Kyle Vanden Bosch	RE	1999–2000

Kyle Vanden Bosch